PURITAN CHILDREN IN EXILE

The Effects of the Puritan Concepts of the Original Sin, Death, Salvation, and Grace upon the Children and Grandchildren of the Puritan Emigrants leading to the Collapse of the Puritan Period

FOREWORD BY

REVEREND JOYCE LARSON FRAME

EPILOGUE BY

DR. LITA LINZER SCHWARTZ, PSYCHOLOGIST

© GERALD GARTH JOHNSON

January, 2002

Johnson, Gerald Garth
The Puritan Children in Exile: The Effects of the Puritan Concepts of the Original Sin, Death, Salvation, and Grace upon the Children and Grancdchildren of the Puritan Emigrants leading to the Collapse of the Puritan Period.

1. Puritans. 2. Religion. 3. New England. 4. Massachusetts Bay Colony. 5. Colonial Period. 6. Churches. 7. Sermons. 8. Death. 9. Burials. 10. Bible. 11. Children. 12. School. 13. Books. 14. Sin. 15. Grace. 16. Salvation.

Published 2002 by
HERITAGE BOOKS, INC.
1540E Pointer Ridge Place, Bowie, Maryland 20716
1-800-398-7709
www.heritagebooks.com

ISBN 0-7884-2009-7

A Complete Catalog Listing Hundreds of Titles
On History, Genealogy, and Americana
Available Free Upon Request

For

Nancy Anne Ticknor Johnson

and our children

LeAnne, Lisa, and Geoffrey,
and their children

with love

Gerald Garth Johnson, Ph.D. is a retired educator and State of Oregon education and social service program administrator who lives in Salem, Oregon. He is the author of several education, law, and historical non-fiction books, two of which are reflective of his interest in 17th Century America. He holds a Bachelors and Masters Degree in Education from Willamette University, and a Ph.D. in Public Administration from California Western University.

The Epilogue for Johnson's *Puritan Children in Exile* was written by Dr. Lita Linzer Schwartz, Distinguished Professor Emerita of Eduational Psychology and Professor Emerita of Women's Studies at Pennsylvania State University. Dr. Schwartz, who is a Diplomate from the American Board of Forensic Psychology, holds degrees from Vassar College, Temple University, and Bryn Mawr College.

Dr. Schwartz is the author of several books on psychology, cult studies, and other subjects, and is a frequent leader of workshops worldwide. In addition, she has contributed scores of articles to professional magazines as well as served as editor of several books in fields of educational psychology, exceptional children, modern-day cults, religious conversion, child custody, and women's issues.

Her knowledge of childhood and child development adds greatly to the *Puritan Children in Exile* and provides the final and important chapter for this book that examines the history, theology, and psychology of the effects of Puritan upbringing on children in Seventeenth Century New England.

Also by Gerald Garth Johnson

Alan, Lord of Buckenhall

The Johnson Papers, Volumes I and II

The Biography and Genealogy of Captain John Johnson from Roxbury, Massachusetts

The Ancestors and Descendants of Ira Johnson and Abigail Furbush Johnson

The Oregon Book of Juvenile Issues

Post-High School Planning

The Stage-Curtis Genealogy

Understanding the Alcoholism in Your Family and Its Effect on You

A Family Portrait in Letters, 1839-1923

The Ticknor Family in America, Supplement

Textual Note: In cases where quoted passages, especially from religious works, diaries, sermons, and poetry, seemed ambiguous because of spelling and punctuation of the Seventeenth Century, these have been changed to modern spelling and punctuation. Further, in cases where the meaning of a word is needed for clarification, the meaning has been added within brackets.

Ye Holy Angels Bright

Ye holy angels bright, who wait at God's right hand, Or through the realms of light Fly at your Lord's command, Assist our song, For else the theme Too high doth seem For mortal tongue.

Ye blessed souls at rest, Who ran this earthly race And now, from sin released, Behold the Saviour's face, God's praises sound, As in his sight With sweet delight Ye do abound.

Ye saints, who toil below, Adore your heavenly King, And onward as ye go Some joyful anthem sing; Take what he gives And praise him still, Through good or ill Who ever lives!

My soul, bear thou thy part, Triumph in God above: And with a well-tuned heart Sing thou the songs of love! Let all thy days Till life shall end, Whate'er he send, Be filled with praise.

Words by Reverend Richard Baxter [1615-1691]

Written 1672 (public domain)

[Note: John Darwall, 1770, put Reverend Richard Baxter's poem to music as an Anglican Hymn.]

THE PURITAN CHILDREN IN EXILE

CONTENTS

CONTENTS – Continued

FOREWORD

As a pastor, one of the questions I am often asked by parents in the church is, "How can we pass on our faith and our values to our children in a healthy, life-affirming way?" As a congregation we are continually challenged with developing and nurturing the spiritual journey of our children, so that they will come to value a personal relationship with Jesus Christ and continue to grow in their spiritual lives beyond childhood and into their adult lives. How do our beliefs, doctrines, and our religious practices enhance or prohibit our children into spiritual wholeness?

Gerald Garth Johnson invites readers to address these questions in this examination of the world of Puritanism, with its practices and believes, in regard to their psychological effects upon the children and grandchildren of the Emigrants. One of Dr. Johnson's premises is that how our society understands and treats its children is central to expected outcomes. The Puritans' alleged harsh, aloof, and strict parenting practices toward their children may have contributed to the lack of interest by the children in pursuing a conversion experience in order to become members of the Church.

Religious practices, in particular, during the Puritan era strived to bring the colonists to a more godly being. Examined from a distance of more than three hundred years, it has become clearer that the negative and punitive efforts of the Calvinist Church Divines and Magistrates at the time had virtually little effect upon the godliness of the adult citizens of the Bay Colony. Likewise, their children and grandchildren were not able to maintain the religious zeal of their forefathers and quickly abandoned many of the Calvinistic views when it became possible in the latter part of the Seventeenth Century.

The reasons for the decline of the Puritan era are many. While the citizens of the Massachusetts Bay Colony were moving (albeit slowly) toward an American Society, the Seventeenth Century clergy never gave up hope for a community of saints. But the lack of having a connection to the world by the Puritan Church Divines is a message that all of us who care for and minister to our neighbors as well as ourselves need to know and understand.

Doctor Johnson's text on Puritan religious practices is an outstanding primer on the subject of religious influence to which we need to listen.

Reverend Joyce Larson Frame

PREFACE

In 1999 upon the completion of a biography of an ancestor, Captain John Johnson from Roxbury, Massachusetts (1630-1659), I became intrigued with two things: first, a listing of ninety books John Johnson loaned to Reverend Richard Mather in 1647 and, second, whether or not the decline of the Puritan Period was based upon any psychological and emotional problems leading to dissatisfaction of the Puritan way by the Puritan children and grandchildren of the Emigrant Founders.

Research has revealed more than I bargained for. The causes of the failure of the Puritans are attributed by some writers of the Early America period to economic issues, land acquisitions, pursuit of individual freedom, and religious diversity (if not toleration), however, there has been found a large body of evidence of abuses and problems of the second and third Puritan generations that may have sped up the removal of the Puritan chokehold on the Massachusetts Bay Colony. Perhaps Reverend Roger Williams said it best that the [Puritans'] "city on a hill was a flawed experiment."

It is hoped that this book gives a voice and importance to the children and grandchildren of the Puritan emigrants. It is through their eyes and experiences that we can learn about the fall of the Puritans.

It is always a pleasure to express gratitude and appreciation to those who have made the road to research and understanding not only easier, but more meaningful. I am utterly amazed from whence comes the help. The taxi driver in Baltimore named Ma'hud, an Egyptian Islamic, gave me a 40-minute discourse on the religion of Islam as we dashed from highways to freeways on the way to Bowie, Maryland. He increased my knowledge of "God."

I am also thankful for meeting Reverend Bruce Wenigmann, Salem, Oregon who suggested several resources that became important to my understanding of Puritanism, fundamentalists, restrictive religious organizations, and the Reformed Churches.

Also extremely helpful was Dr. Lane McGaughy, Willamette University, Salem, Oregon, a truly godly man, who introduced me to the *Geneva Bible* and its implications for the Puritan beliefs and practices who cordially and graciously advised me on sections of this book. Dr. McGaughy is an exceptionally knowledgeable person about religion.

Lastly, I am extremely grateful and indebted to Dr. Lita Linzer Schwartz, psychologist, who edited this book. In addition, she politely and enthusiastically pointed me toward resource material and away from quick conclusions that could not be supported. Her Epilogue to this book brings everything in this book into focus and perspective.

Gerald F. Moran and Maris A. Vinovskis in their William and Mary Quarterly [1982] article, "The Puritan Family and Religion: A Critical Reappraisal" suggests that "inquiry into the relationship of family and religion not only employ or test unconventional methods of research---but recover the fundamentals of human experience in past time." [1]

I could not agree more with Moran and Vinovskis. But more important in my estimation is the examination of the effect of family and religion on the successive generations and what effect the emigrant family and its religion had on the mental health of the children and grandchildren. Modernization of the family depends upon discarding values and things that no longer are acceptable or defensible. Clearly, the families between 1630 and 1830 progressed ahead, perhaps haltingly, to represent a modernization that this Century's families now experience, for better or for worse.

As Americans rushing through the new millennium, we may view our history in America and the legacies of that history, as too far back to matter. Yet, the three hundred-seventy years since the Puritans landed in the Bay in what is now known as Salem, Massachusetts is not such a great distance back historically speaking. The ways the Emigrant founders' children and grandchildren were affected by the Puritans brings new insight into the place of children in our society and their future, is important for us to know.

Gerald Garth Johnson, Ph.D.
Salem, Oregon
November 2001

ACKNOWLEDGMENTS

Most of this book was written over a ten-month period beginning in the year 2000. I was fortunate in the initial stages of researching to have had access to Oregon's research and federal depository library, the University of Oregon Knight Memorial Library in Eugene, Oregon. I received excellent assistance from the library staffs at Willamette University Mark O. Hatfield Library in Salem, Oregon and the Paul L. Boley Library at the Northwest School of Law at Lewis and Clark College in Portland, Oregon.

Extremely important in the research for this study were the weeks spent at Yale University, New Haven, Connecticut in the Sterling Memorial Library, the Beinecke Rare Book and Manuscript Library, and the Yale School of Divinity Library. I cannot think of a more professional and competent group of librarians and staff. Their expertise made research a pleasure.

Help also came in various stages and forms during the period of composition. I am so grateful for the advice, comments, and especially the encouragement from family, friends, and professionals in the fields of history, sociology, and theology. Their observations prompted me to be thorough in my findings.

Dr. Laird Towle, CEO of Heritage Books, Incorporated has been extremely supportive and encouraging. His belief in the focus of the book has been wonderful.

Dr. George McCowen, Professor Emeritus from Willamette University, Salem, Oregon, deserves acknowledgment and much credit for his resourcefulness. He kept me focused. Likewise, Professor Gail McCowen, Western Oregon University, introduced Medieval History to me that was the heritage of the Puritan thinking, place, and practice about women and children. I am grateful for the McCowens' inspiration and their friendship.

I am also thankful for Simon Skudder of Bristol, England for his assistance in tracking down Seventeenth Century English Imprints of William Bradshaw and Samuel Crook in Bristol and Oxford, England. His letters produced sources for rare book copies of the two authors. Later, we found that they had been filmed and were in the Early British Imprints collection available here in America!

Nickole A. Quackenbush of *Q Consulting,* Salem, Oregon, not only helped me take command of Microsoft Word and my computer but helped with formatting issues during my "periods of frustration." Her expert final copy editing for publication of needed page breaks, as well as guide me through the process of endnotes, and assisting me with the index was very helpful. Her cheerful, competent, and resourceful assistance is gratefully appreciated and acknowledged. I could not have completed this final document without her.

INTRODUCTION

The author's recent completion of *The Biography and Genealogy of Captain John Johnson from Roxbury, Massachusetts* raised considerably more questions than it answered about the Puritans between 1630 and 1670. Considering the limited number of inhabitants in New England in those years, probably no other group, before or after the Puritans, has received as much scrutiny, admiration, and criticism. "Puritan" is used throughout this book to identify the people who came to the Massachusetts Bay Colony from the 1630 landing of the *Arbella* and its sister ships commonly called the Winthrop Fleet to those who came later out of rejection of the English Church. But as Stephen Foster wrote in his introduction to *Their Solitary Way* published by the Yale University Press in 1971, "Winthrop and the others on the *Arbella* would not have used the label "Puritan," but they did admit to advocating a thoroughgoing reformation [purification] of the church and society in their native England." [2] Foster continues that the group called the Puritans believed "they were simply the most important body of people since the Apostles." [3]

Regardless, "Puritan" has become the nomenclature and has been used by most historians for the thousands of people who came to Massachusetts and other areas between 1630-1670 even though it may not be the most accurate labeling.

In the thousands of books and articles written over the past three hundred and seventy years about the Puritans, the reasons for the failure of the Puritan movement have been attributed variously to desire for democracy, lack of democracy, economic conditions, religious war in England, restoration of the monarchy, and on and on.

None of the above reasons necessarily are wrong. However, it is the belief of this author that the real answers for the fall of the Puritans are in deeply rooted religious beliefs and practices that were neither acceptable nor hopeful to the children and grandchildren of the emigrant founders. These children and grandchildren did not have membership in the local Churches in the Massachusetts Bay Colony, and their doubts, fears, anxieties, hopelessness, and concerns about their lives and their souls were not addressed by the Colony nor by their parents and grandparents.

This study of the Puritan concepts of Original Sin, Death, Salvation, Free Will, and Grace examines the Halfway Covenant, sin, laws, death, burial rites and burial sermons, Salvation, and Grace as well as the literal Bible interpretations. The discussion of the "Elect Saints" of the Church adds new archival information heretofore not considered as reasons for the declination of the "New Israel."

Much of the focus of this book is on the beliefs about the place of children and the parenting practices provided for these disenfranchised children. One can only imagine what affect the aloofness of the Puritan parent had on the attitudes and future beliefs and parenting skills of the Puritan children and grandchildren. It must be remembered, as J. I. Packer cited in *A Quest for Godliness: The Puritan Vision of the Christian,* Puritans were obedient to the Church Divines because [even] "the Puritan preacher regarded himself as the mouthpiece of God and servant of His words." [4]

Considering the strong allegiance of the "Elect Saints" to their Preachers and their religion that did not give children respect and a place in society, it is no wonder the second and third generation children rejected the "Puritan Way" once they became adults. Democracy, as it grew to be conceived by

1776, initiated the process of providing individual rights and freedoms practically unknown to the world's population at that time.

Included in the *Appendix* are important documents of the Seventeenth Century that can provide insight into the heart and soul of the Puritan emigrants. The *Catechism*, for example, by Reverend John Cotton, relates the vigorous religious learning that was required of all children at an early age. *Spiritual Milk for Babes Drawn Out of the Breasts of Both Testaments for Their Souls Nourishment* was a document used in school as a supplement to the *New England Primer*. Also included in the *Appendix* is a *List of Ninety Books Borrowed by Reverend Richard Mather in 1647* from Captain John Johnson of Roxbury, Massachusetts. This inclusion of the ninety religious books of Johnson's indicates that not only could Johnson read Latin and English, but as a layman, he was well-informed about his faith.

The *Massachusetts Body of Liberties (1641)* provides a clear example of the types of laws that eventually were needed since faith alone did not address all justice and social issues.

Thomas Weld's *Heresies of Anne Hutchinson and Her Followers* reveals as much about Weld as it does about Hutchinson. It is important, too, as to clarifying what the place of women was in the Puritan Seventeenth Century.

It has been possible to follow the sermonizing and practices of four successive pastors in the Massachusetts Bay Colony covering a period of sixty years. By including the beliefs of Puritan tolerationists Rev. Roger Williams, Anne Hutchinson, and other more liberal pastors and townsmen, readers can finally begin to capture the essence of the Puritan dilemma faced by the second and third generations of Puritans who felt *exiled* from the Church and the Puritan society of their ancestors.

While the concentration of this book is on the human concern with one's future…alive and dead, it is just one of a thousand books about the Puritans, and has been designed to bring additional inquiry and information through scholarly research to the issues related to the Puritans, instead of providing answers to end all the doubt and concern.

The religious beliefs, actions, practices, and theocratic ideas of the Seventeenth Century Puritans are examined in this book separate from Puritanism as a whole. There are probably larger studies yet to come from scholars in the field of Early America History, and those can help us build a more effective study and understanding of this population, one by one.

The Puritan lack of self, even the lack of recreation for rejuvenation of the self [as well as the soul] is exposed parallel to the expansion of the expression of thought and the exploration of self-indulgences [sinful or not].

Also, there is an opportunity to reflect upon the beliefs and practices of today's American society in relationship to that of the Puritans. The Puritans and their Old Testament standards have left us unfortunate legacies that some, such as Bible literalists, as well as other restrictive religious groups are not inclined to abandon in the very near future. The evidence is clear, however, that children are negatively impacted by these held over Puritan legacies.

Because of the wide variety of individual and community practices, the focus of this book is primarily Suffolk County, Massachusetts. It is felt that a wider area would have brought in variants that would skew the conclusions too generally. [For example, childrearing practices in Springfield, Massachusetts could have been different from those in Boston because Springfield was distanced away from the control of the Church Divines and the seat of government.]

While the chapters could be read as 'stand alone' chapters, they were purposely placed in sequential order so that they would lead up to the conclusive remarks by Dr. Lita Linzer Schwartz in the Epilogue.

The examination and exposure of all aspects of death and the ramifications of the emotional and psychological damage to the Puritan children and grandchildren, and its legacy and impact for the future generations, justifies this exploration.

CHAPTER ONE

THE HISTORY OF CONCEPT OF ORIGINAL SIN

The concept of original sin by the Puritans was a cornerstone of their theological foundation and practice. Covenants of grace and works were the others. Since Adam betrayed God and his subsequent fall for his transgressions, children and all people were singled out as inheritors of Adam's sin.

The Puritans, while rejecting Roman Catholic theology and practices, retained more of the Roman doctrines and concepts than they were able to admit. Protestants, in general, embraced the Augustine (354-430 A.D.) notion that

> "Adam's fall [sin] from grace had left
> humanity inheritently [sic] flawed, incapable
> of acting correctly, and thus entirely dependent
> upon God's mercy." [5]

Augustine, although well-intended, developed his "original sin" theory in the Fifth Century about how sin was carried forward to each generation.

It did not take long for early Western Christians to begin the belief that "original sin" was passed down from generation to generation through sexual intercourse. [Some Fundamentalists and Pentecostals still believe that sex itself was the original sin.]

As Augustine said, "This diabolical excitement of the genitals is evidence of Adam's original sin which is now transmitted from the mother's womb tainting all human beings with sin, and leaving them incapable of choosing good over evil or determining their own destiny." [6]

1

Augustine's doctrine provides us with his view of an inflexible God as indicated in the following passage:

> "Banished [from Paradise] after his sin, Adam bound his offspring also with the penalty of death and damnation, that offspring which by sinning he had corrupted in himself, as in a root; so that whatever progeny was born through carnal concupiscence, by which a fitting retribution for his disobedience was bestowed upon him from himself and his spouse---who was the cause of his sin and the companion of his damnation---would drag through the ages the burden of Original Sin, by which it would itself be dragged through manifold errors and sorrows, down to that final and never-ending torment with the rebel angels. . So the matter stood; the damned lump of humanity was lying prostrate, no, was wallowing in evil, it was falling headlong from one wickedness to another; and joined to the faction of the angels who had sinned, it was paying the most righteous penalty of its impious treason." [7]

While Early Christians for several Centuries had considered the sexual act as sinful for all purposes except procreation, it did not take John Calvin and later Puritans of England and New England long to reject sexual pleasure.

Of course, the Puritans like all human beings, could not resist the pleasure of having sexual intercourse. The remorse, however, was real and with every child conceived, the Puritans knew that the "original sin" had been committed and passed on.

It needs to be established that Muslims, Jews, and Orthodox Christians did not regard the theology of "original sin" in the same way as the West did.

According to Bishop John Spong (Ret.) in *Why Christianity Must Change or Die*, the Biblical narrative in Genesis about Adam and Eve established that "the perfection of creation was ruined" by the eating of the forbidden fruit. [8] Because of this first sin by Adam and Eve, human life was to be lived in pain, suffering, struggles, and death. The Puritans truly believed this theology and further believed that death was the consequence of sinning. This concept was, in turn, part of what every Puritan child learned early on. [See Chapter Six on "Death, Heaven, and Hell] Death was punishment for sins!

Apostle Paul, (in 1 Cor. 15:22) said,

> "For as in Adam all die, so also in Christ shall all be made alive."

Augustine, a later theologian than Apostle Paul, firmly established that at least for the Western world, Jesus Christ would provide redemption [atonement] for the sins of man.

As foreign and as difficult it may seem to Bible literalists, the New Testament and its interpretations by Augustine, Thomas of Aquinas, and others were developed over *hundreds and hundreds of years.*

Some of what we believe in the Twenty-first Century are doctrines, ideas, and theology that were written by Early Church leaders. These doctrines, written to provide understanding and clarity, ended up benefiting as well as establishing the place of the Roman Catholic Church.

Augustine in the Fourth Century, for example, worked out the whole idea of the virgin birth since his belief was that inasmuch as sin was passed on from generation to generation, it had to be established that redemption by Jesus Christ could be made more acceptable to his generation [and future ones] if Jesus was portrayed as not being a descendant of Adam, the progenitor of sin. Jesus, as a son of the Holy Spirit of God, was not tainted by the original sin and his redemptive promises were intact.

It was not until the 1800s that the Roman Catholic Church developed the doctrine of the Immaculate Conception of the Blessed Virgin. Now that Mary was freed of the burden of the sin of Adam, Jesus then was not fully qualified to provide atonement for sins of man. He was perfectly pure.

Moreover, "From about 80 CE to the present time, most faith groups within the Christian religion have taught that Jesus was conceived by his mother Mary before she engaged in sexual intercourse. The Holy Spirit accomplished this conception without any physical act. Faith groups include Anglican, Eastern Orthodoxy, Protestantism, and Roman Catholicism. This doctrine is usually called the virgin birth. It has long been one of the Roman Catholic Church's foundation beliefs. And, the Church creeds have mentioned it as well." [9] However, liberal theologians do not support this concept any longer.

Furthermore, the notion of the Immaculate Conception is mainly a Roman Catholic doctrine. It is unrelated to the virgin conception and birth, but is often confused with it. Most people seem to believe that the dogma of the Immaculate Conception declares that Jesus was without original sin when Mary conceived him. In fact, it is really the belief that about 20 BCE when Mary herself was conceived that she was without original sin. It is required belief for Roman Catholics.

In 1854, Pope Pius IX proclaimed in his *Bull Infalibis* that "...we declare, pronounce and define that the doctrine which asserts that the Blessed Virgin Mary, from the first moment of her conception, by a singular grace and privilege of Almighty God, and in view of the merits of Jesus Christ, savior of the human race, was preserved free from every stain of original sin is a doctrine revealed by God and, for this reason, must be firmly and constantly believed by all the [Catholic] faithful." [10] This is not the teaching in the Eastern Orthodox Church, in the Anglican Community, nor any Protestant denomination.

The Puritans, convinced that the original sin was a burden to carry, spent all of their lives in repentance never truly understanding the history of the Roman Catholic Church.

Children were reminded of their vicarious nature by statements such as:

Augustine:

> "From this condemnation, no one is exempt, not even children." [11]

> "Children are infected by parents' sins as well as Adam's and the actual sins of the parents impose guilt upon the children." [12]

> "Whatever offspring is born is bound to sin." [13]

And, from Reverend John Calvin, the so-called "father of Puritanism":

> "Original sin is the hereditary depravity and corruption of our nature...which first makes us subject to the wrath of God, and then produces in us works which the Scriptures call works of the flesh."

> "The sin of Adam is the immediate cause and ground of inborn depravity, guilt and condemnation to the whole human race." [14]

> There is no comfort to children in "the imagination of man's heart is evil from his youth." (Gen. 8:21). Nor in Rom. 3:23, "All have sinned and come short of the glory of God."

> "Ye shall not add unto the word which I command you, neither shall diminish aught from it..." (Deut. 4:2).

It seems in the attempts of the Apostles and other writers of the New Testament to interpret the word, they added to it instead!

And the Puritan preachers, well after the Halfway covenant that allowed Church membership to young people in 1662, continued their disdain for the young as exampled below:

> "You are a little wretched despicable creature; a worm, a mere nothing, and less than nothing; a vile insect, that has risen up in contempt against the majority of heaven and earth." [15]

Interpretations of the Bible by Early Christian clergy as well as modern-day priests and preachers have "added unto the word" therefore, leaving the door open not only for suspicion but errors.

The Calvinistic Puritans held that the sin of Adam thoroughly stained them. Even after 1740, the opposite view of John Taylor of Norwich about Adam's sin not being passed down generation to generation, was not widely accepted or adopted until after 1800.

In an anonymous 1757 tract attributed to Samuel Webster entitled "A Winter Evening's Conversation Upon the Doctrine of Original Sin" questions:

> "[If] myriads of infants...tormented with fire and brimstone, weltering in a lake of flame, suffering a black doom, how could the supreme being be good if responsible for such barbarities?" [16] [because of original sin and damnation]

Unfortunately for the second and third generation children and grandchildren of the Emigrant Founders, Webster was too late [1750s] for a more positive outlook regarding original sin. Even a rebuttal by staunch Puritan Divine Reverend Peter Clark could not stem the tide of questions about the psychological, social and theological weaknesses of the Puritan Way that had been begun by Webster. While attending Harvard College between 1667-1671, Samuel Sewell chose as a Master's thesis the theory, "Is Original Sin Both Sin and Punishment?" Despite all his scriptural learning, "Sewall answered in the affirmative." [17] Sewell eventually softened his viewpoints about religion and justice.

Various versions of the original sin issues were defended up through the First Great Awakening led by Rev. Jonathan Edwards. However, challenges by the Puritans to the more

7

liberal interpretation regarding original sin, especially as applied to children, were interrupted by the Revolution in America...but not forgotten.

Even in the First Great Awakening, while not a major focus of this book, in the sermon and discourse *Sinners in the Hands of an Angry God*, written by Reverend Jonathan Edwards, unconverted persons in the congregation was supposed to be awakened the need for salvation. "This that you have heard is the case of everyone of you that are out of Christ. That world of misery, that lake of burning brimstone is extended abroad to you. There is the dreadful pit of the glowing flames of the wrath of God; there is hell's wide gaping mouth open..." [18]

Jonathan Edwards (1703-58) has been described by the editors in their *A Jonathan Edwards Reader,* as "Colonial America's greatest theologian and philosopher." [19] While Edwards have had many attributes such as vision, writing and preaching skills, and a remarkable interest in science, he used many of the same scare tactics of the Seventeenth Century Puritan Church Divines, and revealed his view of God as one of wrath [not love] and continued the Puritan view of the Roman Catholic Church as the enemy of the "true church" [as defined by Edwards].

The chart below represents the years 1731-1743 of the admission to the First Church of Roxbury that was listed in the *Roxbury Land and Church Records,* published in 1884. [20] The admission statistics do not reflect any particular influence of Jonathan Edwards regarding admissions to the Roxbury church.

Numbers Who Joined the Roxbury Church
1730 – 1743

1730	1731	1732	1733	1734	1735	1736
2	1	4	11	5	2	4

1737	1738	1739	1740	1741	1742	1743
5	1	2	6	6	7	1

Reverend Nehemiah Walter was pastor of the Roxbury Church for the period cited above.

Perhaps Edwards should be best remembered as an important religious figure whose return to Puritan spiritual thought and practice about sin, tried to save the unconverted souls in New England. After all, children were reminded in 1740 by Edwards in "The Justice of God in the Damnation of Sinners" that *"You are a little, wretched, despicable creature; a worm, a mere nothing, and less than nothing; a vile insect, that has risen up in contempt against the majesty of heaven and earth."* [21] These do not sound like words of a "great theologian," and suggests a return to a concept of fear, belittlement, and shame in times past.

Attempts to defend Calvinistic views about original sin continued until well after the Second Great Awakening in the 1840s.

CHAPTER TWO

THE PURITAN CONCEPT OF SIN

As Andrew Delbanco said in *The Puritan Ordeal,* "Puritanism held out the promising of reversing one's slippage in status [into sin]; it gave voice to those who felt discarded from lives of property and ease." [22]

The concept of sin had changed from the outward and obvious sins of fornication, adultery, blasphemy and crimes against the community to sins of the inward and outward person.

John Downame, a respected theologian from whom the Puritans sought strength for their moralistic convictions, was quick to point out that sin was lust and something that the Puritans addressed effectively [for awhile] in the Commonwealth of Massachusetts Bay. (Downame, as below)

Downame continued, "The second enemy which assisteth Satan against us, is the flesh... [who] may easily send whole troupes of temptations to enter and surprise us...it fighteth and lusteth against the spirit...our minds...and leadeth us captive to the laws of sinne..." [23]

With confidence and assuredness, Downame instructed his readers about Satan and man by saying, "Whereof it cometh to pass that Satan wanteth no opportunitie of circumventing us, because we can put no difference between his [Satan] temptations and our owne carnall desires..." [24]

Reverend Richard Sibbes, another important Puritan theologian, and one whose books were consulted by

Reverend Richard Mather and other people in the Colony, emphasized that "sin" was not an entity in itself yet the Puritans created a commonwealth where "sin" was addressed in the family, the Church, and the government.

The emigration and flight from the so-called sinful environs of Old England led to a New England that resembled Old England in nearly every aspect---including sinfulness. The Puritans could not escape the advice of William Perkins in *The Order of the Causes of Salvation and Damnation (1608)* when he concluded, "But everyman is tempted, when he is drawn away of his own lust, and enticed. Then when lust hath conceived, it bringeth forth sin; and sin, when it is finished, bringeth forth death." [25]

Dr. Francis J. Bremer, Professor of History at Millersville University in Pennsylvania, said it best in *The Puritan Experiment* that "the Puritans looked into his heart and saw evil, looked at his behavior and saw sin." [26]

How did the Puritans propose to awaken men, women, and children to their sinful nature and the promise of grace and forgiveness? By sermons! And sermons they did have.

Reverend Nehemiah Walter, the third pastor of the First Church of Roxbury, told his congregation in July, 1706, that "Every Godly Man has Sin dwelling in him. All Men have a corrupt Nature handed down to them from our first Parents." [27]

Walter did not provide much hope for the Elect either. In fact, his entire sermon was actually directed at the "godly" telling them, "Indwelling sin is the root of all actual sins. All the Sins of our Lives proceed from the Sin of our Nature...Indwelling Sin is that which does the *Saints* most Hurt." [28]

Even Native Americans the Puritans who called Indians, did not escape sin. Reverend John Eliot in *New England's First Fruits with Divers Other Special matters Concerning that Country,* stated:

> "Divers of the Indian Children, boyes and girles we have received into our houses, who are long since civilized, and in subjection to us, painfull and handy in their business, and can speak our language familiarly; divers of whom can read English, and begin to understand in their measure, the grounds of Christian Religion; some of them are able to give us Account of the Sermons they hear, and of the word read and expounded in our Families, and are convinced of their sinfull and miserable estates, and affected with the sense of God's displeasure...yet mistake us not we are wont to keep them at such a distance, (knowing they serve the Devil and are led by him...)" [29]

One of the ways Reverend Nehemiah Walter suggested to the Roxbury Church congregation to be "delivered' from sin was to give up being "lovers of pleasures more than lovers of God" and to "wail and be sorrowful in our lamentations as we ask for forgiveness." [30]

Basically, Walter chided his congregation in his 1706 sermon that if they did not have a sorrowful sense of their corruptions, they will never be willing to part with them. He pleaded, "Go to Jesus Christ for Eye-Salve to anoint you, that you may see your selves wretched, and miserable, and poor, and blind, and naked, Rev. 3: 17-18." [31]

Puritans easily made the transition from original sin to represent "all evil." They believed that every sin, actual and

13

original, was a transgression against the laws of God and was contrary to it. (1 John 3:4) Sin made the Puritan subjected to death with all miseries, spiritual, temporal, and eternal.

The Puritans, shortly after their arrival in 1630, had developed laws for the Massachusetts Bay Colony that paralleled the authority of the Scriptures. (See Chapter Five: Puritan Sin and Bible-based Laws) Puritans viewed the Scripture to be God, as the FATHER, speaking to them as if they were children. God's law [the Scriptures] was above all law and anything else was considered to be products of sinful men.

Thomas Watson, author of *The Mischief of Sin,* cites the Psalms as setting down the sins of the people of Israel [likewise, the people of the "New Israel," the Massachusetts Bay Colony]:

Simply, the four major sins he cites from the Psalms are:

    1. forgetting God;

    2. inordinate lusting;

    3. idolatry; and

    4. infidelity. [32]

Watson was certain that sin "brought a person low." And, were brought low for their iniquity. (Psalm 106:43)

Further, Reverend Thomas Watson listed how many ways sin brings a man low:

    1. Sin brings a man low in God's esteem.

2. Sin brings a man low in his intellectual parts.

3. Sin brings a man low in affliction.

4. Sin brings a man low in spiritual plagues.

5. Sin brings a man low in temptation.

6. Sin brings a man low in melancholy.

7. Sin brings a man low in desertion.

8. Sin brings a man low in despair.

9. Sin brings a man without repentance into the bottomless pit, and then he is brought low indeed. [33]

Watson, more than most Puritan writers except Reverend John Cotton, literally detailed every aspect of sin, torments of hell, severity of hell, grace, and how to ward off sin. If *The Mischief of Sin* was written just prior to the 1671 publication date, then we have some evidence that there was neglect in family worship because there was no reading of the Scriptures and no praying. Likewise, there was a decline in keeping the Sabbath Day holy. Adultery was a main sin that was a costly sin and one that hastened one's death. As Watson said, "The adulterer takes a short cut to hell." [34]

But the worst was yet to come. Watson, in his best judgment, pointed out reasons why some sinners should receive [the] greater damnation. Sinners who should receive greater damnation were those such as: [35]

1. are willfully ignorant;

2. will neither follow the thing that is good for themselves, nor yet allow others;

3. sin again clear illuminations and convictions;

4. are plotters and contrivers of sin;

5. are haters of holiness;

6. are lovers of sin;

7. they who shall have a greater degree of torment who persecuted the saints of the Most High;

8. are seemingly good so that they may be really bad, who make profession a specious presence for their wickedness so that, under this mask, they may lie and deceive;

9. such as do no works of mercy;

10. die under final unbelief;

11. have grown gray under the gospel but are never the better;

12. die with the falling sickness, who apostatize and fall away from the truth;

13. Ishmael spirits as scoff at religion;

14. have perverted others by their corrupt writings;

15. make their bodies vessels of uncleanness; and

16. send other men to hell by their bad example.

Paul Pierson, in Audio Tape 12 of *Historical Development of the Christian Movement*, remarked that the Puritans thought "every person a sinner, but every person has full potential to be the child of God and full human being." [36]

Pierson suggests that the Puritans saw themselves engaged in warfare against evil. Indeed, many of the Puritan writers like Downame, Sibbes, Preston, Rogers and others had written works called "Christian Warfare" or similar titles.

The "warfare" was tough work. Conversion was the ONLY way out of damnation and "anyone who had not been redeemed by conversion was reckoned to be still outside." [37] [the fold of Christ.]

According to Dr. Sanford Fleming in *Children and Puritanism*, the "result of all this was that there was an exaggerated emphasis upon an austere view of life. Young and old were exhorted to think of death [because of sin] rather than life, and in innumerable ways the "otherworldly attitude [sin] was fostered." [38]

But the "war" against the types of evil in the Seventeenth Century by the Puritans were quite similar to those sins identified in the *"Pauline Epistles"* as early as the Second Century and even the same types of sins experienced in Old England prior to emigration. These Epistles are named for Apostle Paul's thirteen letters drawn from Paul's writings now contained in Romans, 1 and 2 Corinthians, Galatians, Ephesians, Philippians, Colossians, 1 and 2 Thessalonians, 1 and 2 Timothy, Titus and Philemon. [Note: Some theologians believe Ephesians, Colossians, 2 Thessalonians, and 1 Timothy, may not be the writing of Paul. However, inclusion of them as they pertain to this chapter on the Puritan Concept of Sin would change by removing the above-named letters.]

The Seven Deadly Sins from the *Pauline Epistles* are:

1. Pride

2. Avarice (Miserly)

3. Envy

4. Anger

5. Laziness

6. Lust

7. Gluttony

The Puritan believed that every written word in Paul's letters was for the Puritan and his learning.

In addition to the Seven Deadly Sins as well as Watson's lists of sins, the Puritans went about making many things and activities "sinful" some of which also carried a criminal punishment.

From a variety of sources, some of the "common-day sins" of the Puritans and non-Puritans alike are listed from Oberholzer, Powell, Greven, Cotton, Morgan, Delbanco, and others:

> Swearing, premarital sex, homosexuality, sex with animals, adultery, lusting, desiring or obtaining wealth, not observing the Sabbath Day, celebrating Christmas, drunkenness, uncleanness, incest with a family member, deceitfulness, not covering one's arms [with sleeves], lying, believing in more than one God,

gambling, murder, strolling in a village on a Sunday, excesses of every kind, men wearing long hair, smoking in the street, dating without consent of the girl's parents, kissing in public, witchcraft, consulting with a witch, tolerating other religions, heresy, perjury, betraying the country, reviling the Magistrates and Governor, sexual intercourse with a virgin maid, whoredom of a maiden in her father's house kept secret, stealing, false witness, maiming or wounding of a free man, slander, premeditated malice, hatred or cruelty, kidnapping, unreasonable prices, and playing of shuffleboard.

Some of the above "sins" are still considered unlawful in some societies, and are followed by believers in certain religious groups as well as by customs of various countries and regions.

Reverend Richard Sibbes, a Seventeenth Century theologian for whom the Puritans had great admiration and respect, assured Puritans and other readers that, "God justified Christ from our sins, being our surity, taking our sins upon him. We are justified, because he by his resurrection quit himself from the guilt of our sins, *as having paid the debt for us.* [39] [italics added]

The Puritans probably believed Sibbes' assurances about Christ having paid the peoples' debt for sin by His death, but they saw an obligation to rid the entire Colony of sinful activities.

Application of penalties for sinning was not applied equally or fairly. Men were treated more fairly than women; the more wealthy, better than the poorer.

Sin was considered a miserable condition for the Puritans, and the Puritan Divines told their congregations over and over that only those who were sinless would avoid going to Hell.

Public condemnation, fines, hangings, and whipping posts were merely outward proof of the sinful nature of man. Reverend Cotton Mather's advise to Puritan parents was strong:

> "Charge them to avoid the snares of Evil Company. Terrify them with warnings of those Deadly Snares. Often repeat the Charge unto them, That if there be any Vicious Company, they shun them, as they would the Plague or the Devil." [40]

Some Puritan Divines like Thomas Weld(e) of the First Church of Roxbury, Massachusetts have been identified as preaching primarily to the non-sinners and the children. This may be, but the terror and fear instilled in the non-believer, the non-saint, and the non-saint children had little effect on their conversion to Jesus Christ and did not result in any noticeable reduction of sin between 1630 and 1700 in the Massachusetts Bay Colony.

The Puritans condemned the celebration of the Church of England holy days because of the inclusion of pagan, non-Christian activities of sex and alcohol. Puritans were firmly against any event that was contrary to their belief that sporting events and holy days, as examples [whether including sex and alcohol or not], had no place in the life of a good Christian.

Massachusetts Bay Colony children were also reprimanded for any type of play or sports. Bruce C. Daniels in *Puritans*

20

at Play, confirms that "no sports took place in the founding generation, and, surprisingly, few in the next hundred years." [41]

Parents were challenged by the Puritan Divines to bring children up in a Godly way. [Note: The long-term effect was that if a "Visible Saint" brought a child up correctly then the child would be sinless and a Visible Saint. Likewise, the grandchild of the Emigrant Founder, if raised correctly and Godly would also be a sinless, Visible Saint. It did not work that way, however.]

Though the mother of Joseph Porter of Salem, Massachusetts, who apparently did not "raise her son correctly or godly," pleaded with the Court to have justice toward her son. In March of 1664, Joseph Porter was sentenced to stand in the gallows and then to be whipped, imprisoned, and fined for slandering his mother by calling his mother "rambeggar, gammar [meaning "old"] shithouse, gammar pisshouse, gammar two shoes, and told her [that] her tongue went like a peare monger." [42]

In reality, Joseph Porter could have been hanged for his disobedience for the Massachusetts Bay laws required death of rebellious and stubborn children based upon the Bible in Deuteronomy 22:20, 21. [The Puritans never used this law although it was in their law books until the mid-1700s.]

The mother [and father] of Joseph Porter could have faced discipline, too, for not "raising or correcting" their child. But this event happened in 1664, not 1630, so it is assumed that the Magistrates were more lenient and more respectful of a mother's request for justice.

In spite of frank discussions about lawful sex and sexual sins by the Puritan "fathers," they felt uneasy to say the least. They just could not conceive that sexual desire was not something that would test their resolve for purity nor was it something that would destroy the underpinnings of their religion. Puritan men and women were long in coming to believe that sexual experiences were not related to the spiritual experiences and were not directly related to the "Original Sin." It was, of course, the spiritual experiences that counted in their estimation. More often that not, the Puritan Divines used words like "sinful," "filthy," "vile," "unclean" in describing things sexual or body related. The clergy usually lifted up the "body" in discourse as a source of sin that needed to be condemned and punished.

In *ChristianityToday.com,* it is stated that "promiscuity was absent from colonial New England." [43] There appears to be an effort to provide readers a picture of happy, colorful, humorous people who partied and had no sexual hang-ups. However, the research of the Seventeenth Century of the records of Suffolk and Middlesex Counties in Massachusetts suggests just the opposite. Dr. Roger Thompson, for example, from his research of the Counties' records [and reported in *Sex in Middlesex*] that there was significant adultery and sexual promiscuity in New England. In fact, records that Thompson cited clearly establish that the adolescent population in the Seventeenth Century was very promiscuous, and lends support for the notion of an existing adolescent culture similar to any group of adolescents in any century.

Furthermore, Thompson found evidence of "members of thirty-five elite families were convicted of sexual offences, almost all of them extramarital affairs." [44]

Also failing to live up to the rigorous sexual and spiritual requirements of the Emigrant Founders were offspring of Puritan Divines: Mather, Cotton, Eliot, Weld, Ward, and others as well as children of lay leaders Keane, Johnson, Winthrop, Savage, Sewell, Dudley, and the Willoughbies.

According to Dr. Thompson, both the daughter and granddaughter of Captain Edward Johnson [author of *The Wonder Working Providence of Sion's* [Zion's] *Savior*] were found "guilty of fornication as were two sons of President Henry Dunster of Harvard University." [45]

Samuel Gookin, son of Major Daniel Gookin, fathered a bastard child in 1677. Major Goodkin's maid Hannah Brackett, had a baby out of wedlock fathered by John Eliot, a son and grandson of ministers. [Reverend John Eliot, grandfather of John Eliot named above, was preacher at the Roxbury Church and to the Indians.]

Thompson reports that the comparable percentages for sexual offenses in the Seventeenth Century in Middlesex County were:

Fornication	47 percent
Adultery	31 percent
Bride pregnancy	65 percent

Sexual misconduct was spread out overall social classes from the gentry class, Church Divines, civil authorities, and the poorer people as well. The available evidence, contradicting findings of "no promiscuity," provides accurate information about the culture of the Puritan society.

Reverend Cotton Mather agonized yet was divided in regard to his sexual desires. According to Robert Middlekauff in *The Mathers,* Cotton Mather, like most Puritans, "wanted gratification and craved denial." [46] Puritans viewed pain as a message from God for which to be thankful just as they saw joy as requiring punishment for those sinful/joyful experiences in all aspects of their lives.

Cotton Mather never could escape his thoughts about sin. Prior to his death, Mather wrote a discourse called *The Duties of Parents to Their Children.* In reprimanding the parents, he said, "In the Name of God, Look after your own Souls," and "If you do not first become yourselves Pious, you will do nothing to purpose to make your children so." [47]

Mather continues in his discourse to describe children in a "Corrupt Nature in thy children, which is a Fountain of all Wickedness and Confusion." [48]

Parents were reminded by Mather to "Withhold not correction from the Child; for if thou beatest him with the Rod, he shall not die; Thou shalt beat him with the rod, and shall deliver his Soul from Hell." [49]

And his last advice to the Parents [and not terribly comforting to the children] was:

> "Often say, my son, if sinners entice thee, consent thou not. Often say, My Child, walk with the Wise and thou shall be wise but a Companion of Fools shall be destroyed. Oh, Do not let the Beasts of prey, carry away thy children alive." [50]

Cotton Mather did not leave the children out of his instruction about sin. In his *The Duties of **Children** to their Parents,* he advises the children:

> "There was a Law in Israel, Deut. 21:21: that the Rebellious Child should be put to Death.

24

After stoning, he was Hang'd up; for in Israel they Hang'd up none, till they had first otherwise kill'd him; and no doubt, his Corpse being taken down, as it was to be done before Sunset, it was thrown into a Noted Pit, such as one as that, into which they threw the Corpse of Judas over the Precipice; and there the Fowls of Heaven prey'd upon it. Agur perhaps alludes to This: And we often see it so, that the Rebellious Child, is left of God, unto those Crimes, for which he is put to Death, e're it be long.

Maintain in your own Spirits, a Dread of those Dreadful Curses, with which the God of Heaven uses to take Vengeance on the Children, who put not Respect, but Contempt, upon their Parents. Beyond, how dreadfully the Judgments of God follow the Children that Set Light by their parents; and Oh, my Warned Children, upon the sight of those Warnings, cry out, Lord, my Flesh trembles for fear, and I am afraid of those Judgments.

Indeed there is no Sin more usually Revenged, with the Sensible and Notable Curses of God, than that Sin, The Contempt of Parents." [51]

John Owen, an English Puritan, reminded the Puritans that as long as they had "unmortified" sin lurking in their hearts, they were not free from the law's condemnation. A more contemporary preacher, Reverend Joseph Rowlandson, on November 21, 1678, two days before his death at age forty-one, told his congregation that God was about to abandon the Puritans for their sinful nature, but he did provide them a guideline for redemption. Rowlandson, like the Mathers, never changed from the notion of sinfulness and threats of hell as a motivator to change people. Reverend Rowlandson, who preached at Weatherfield, Massachusetts, offered the following list of sins that he said "for which God forsook the Jews and are rise amongst us": [52]

1. Horrid Pride (Hos.5.5)

2. Deep and high Ingratitude (Deut.32.6)

3. Oppression (Amos 8.4)

4. Weariness of God's Ordinances (Amos 8.5)

5. Cousenage in men's dealings (making the shekel [money] great and dishonesty in trade (Amos 8.5,6)

6. Idolatry

7. Incorrigibleness (Jer.5.3 and Jer.7.13)

Rowlandson's list of sins is similar to ones suggested by clergy in the late 1500s and early 1600s. Rowlandson is an example of sermonizing that did not keep pace with the times from the beginning of the Massachusetts Bay Colony until after the removal of the Charter by the English Monarchy.

The purpose of the law, according to Owen, was to reveal sin as utterly sinful in order to arouse and humble the soul.

The *Body of Liberties,* the first Massachusetts Bay Colony set of laws, that reveal sin as utterly sinful and humble the soul, are included in the Appendices. Those laws and penalties related to sin are in the "Capitall laws" section" of the *Body of Liberties* for further examination.

Readers may think it unusual that Cotton Mather and other Puritan Divines gave such energy to things that in the Twenty-first Century would be considered "non-clergy" responsibilities. However, the Puritan people, because of the theocracy, placed great responsibility and respect on the clergy. Sometimes it was difficult to differentiate church from civil. It was after all, a "common [share the] wealth [and the agony."] and the Puritans did not attempt to separate church from community from civil from military.

CHAPTER THREE

CHURCH MEMBERSHIP; VISIBLE SAINTS; ELECT PEOPLE; AND THE EFFECT UPON THE PURITAN CHILDREN

If one of the cornerstones of the Puritan religion was the concept of original sin, then the designation of some of the Puritans as "Visible Saints" was close behind.

Church membership in the Massachusetts Bay Colony was limited to those ADULT Puritans who had a covenant with God and who had confessed their sins.

"Visible Saints" also were known by the names of "Chosen Elect" or "Elect" [from the Book of Revelation]. The Elect Puritans believed that it was their responsibility to God to purify themselves [and be visible saints] as well as purify everyone else who had not embraced the same Bible interpretations.

Nearly all Calvinist [Puritans] opposed universal Church membership. In order for a previously non-Puritan to be granted Church membership, the person had to appear before a group or board of Elders and be examined on three spiritual issues: (1) prove their belief and understanding in the doctrine of John Calvin, (2) prove that they were godly in every aspect, and, (3) demonstrate that they had had a definite experience of conversion.

In the last half of the 1600s, about three-fourths of the population in Massachusetts were non-Puritans. Church membership for the visible saints meant that they could enjoy the sacraments of the Church such as baptism and communion. Once a person gained membership in a church as a visible saint, they could be expected to interpret the will of God and make judgments [sometimes harsh ones] about other emigrants who were not Puritans. There was great controversy regarding baptism as a requirement for communion.

Other faiths such as Judaism, Roman Catholicism, and Anglican [Episcopal] similarly require at least a cursory acknowledgment of what joining the church means. Many Protestant congregations merely require unison acknowledgement of those wishing to join the church by repeating their acceptance of Jesus Christ as their savior, and in some cases, the tenets of that particular church.

Reverend Cotton Mather in 1678 was at first in disagreement with the Brattle Street Church, a liberal Puritan church, regarding baptism and public confession of faith and examination for membership by the minister [rather than a Board of Elders]. Cotton Mather eventually capitulated on these issues [as well as the selection of ministers by the entire congregation].

Furthermore, baptism and communion were possible for children at Brattle Street. The 1662 Halfway Covenant was eliminated by the Battle Street Church and eventually its elimination touched most all of the Puritan Churches by 1750.

Perry Miller in *The New England Mind: From Colony to Province,* said about the Brattle Street Church:

> "the only really revolutionary proposition in the *Gospel Order Revisited* [a Brattle Street Church response to Increase Mather's *The Order of the Gospel*] is its assertion that the doctrine of Church covenant is a stranger to

Scripture, and has no foundation in the Word of God." [53]

By insisting that the New Testament did not prescribe any covenant [presumably to allow for a minority of spiritual thinkers to bring an exclusive, visible saints church into being], the Battle Street Church's statements led to a rationality not known or allowed before.

Miller concluded that Battle Street "made a contribution to what eventually could become democracy." [54]

The significance of not being a visible saint meant that the person could not form his own church and could not be baptized or receive communion. Furthermore, the non-visible saint could not have his children baptized. [Note: Non-Church members could not vote yet were required to attend Church and pay a Church tax.]

Reverend John Cotton and the Mathers, principal spokespersons for the Doctrine of Grace through conversion, never gave up their insistence that the main focus or mission of the Church for the Puritans was for the saved, visible saint and not for the "sinners."

John Eliot, the second Roxbury Church Divine or teacher, used his spare time to convert Indians. Eliot was a bit out of step with his fellow ministers.

Edmund S. Morgan an author on the Early America period and particularly in regard to visible saints, said in his book, *Visible Saints—The History of a Puritan Idea:*

> "In New England, he [John Eliot] and other Puritan ministers continued to exclude from the sacraments all but the proven regenerate

31

[Visible Saints]. In spite of prodding by English Presbyterians and Anglicans, the New Englanders refused to reverse their withdrawal from the world...the New England Churches were eventually brought back to earth, not by corruption of the flesh, but by its biology." [55]

There was recognition and great expectation by Reverend John Cotton and other clergy that each Puritan generation was responsible to carry forward through its offspring, the next generation of church members.

Unfortunately for John Cotton, the Mathers, and other Divines, most children of the Emigrant founders who were Visible Saints, did not receive saving grace and conversion thus could not be admitted to the church as members.

Preaching, the accepted and acknowledged way to generate converts to the church, had failed in the 1650s to produce additional church members. By not having the first generation of children accepted for lack of grace and conversion, the second generation of children [grandchildren of the Emigrant founders] could not join the church. The effect of this oversight by the Emigrant founders and the Church Divines resulted in a rapid decline in church membership.

Children [now adults] who were born in the Church but not full-fledged members, in 1662 were eventually provided a "halfway covenant" as basically was a continuation of the status as was granted when a child.

The 'halfway covenant' discussed in more detail in Chapter Four, did not allow the adult children who had not had a conversion experience, to vote in church affairs and they could not join the Visible Saints at the communion table. They did, however, gain baptism for their children.

This hollow attempt to solve the short-sidedness of the early Puritans resulted in more and more second and third generation "Puritans" leaving the church.

Morgan pointed out in his book that "the New England churches had never admitted the right of a church member to leave a church unless excommunicated [for bad behavior] or formally discharged to another Puritan church." [56]

By 1649, most of the church membership was composed of non-visible saints, so called "unregenerates." Reverend Thomas Shepard, Sr., suggested that "such a church would contain many chaffy hypocrites and oft times prophane (sic) persons." [57] He did not elaborate on the effect the issue of having saints and hypocrites [sinners] at the same time in the church had on the emotional and spiritual wellbeing of the children.

Morgan pointed out that the "decline of piety in the population as a whole and the halfway covenant had nothing to do with the population at large." [58] However, it is strongly suggested that the stringent requirements for halfway and full membership resulted in lower church membership and a higher criminal rate in the Colony.

George E. Ellis in *The Puritan Commonwealth: Its Basis, Organization and Administration,* wrote:

> "Here we note a very natural relation between the spirit of persecution and the spirit which obstinately and even wantonly or perversely provoked it. The fathers were anxiously, we say morbidly and timidly, dreading lest their bold

33

venture in the wilderness should be prostrated before it could strike root...

Their troublers came precisely in the form and shape in which they apprehended them...As will soon appear, there was something extraordinary in the odd variety, the grotesque characteristics, and the specially irritating and exasperating course of that strange succession of men and women, of all sorts of odd opinions and notions, who presented themselves during a period of thirty years, seeming to have in common no other object than to grieve and exasperate the Puritan magistrates." [59]

The uneven application in the Massachusetts Bay Colony of punishment for unacceptable behavior was a dominant factor in determining relationships of cause and effect. Magistrates varied in sentencing because many believed that the offender/sinner would "go to Hell anyway." Nonetheless, there is a compelling rise in deviant behaviors for each decade beginning in 1640 forward. This rate of increase may be only related to the Puritan society's ability to detect deviancy.

The lack of community because of the restrictive nature of church membership may have been the overriding reason the Puritan period came to a rapid end.

CHAPTER FOUR

HALFWAY COVENANT; SYNOD OF 1662

Because of the challenges to religion within and out of the Puritan world, the leaders created and published the *Cambridge Platform of 1648.* This platform basically responded to the concern of Puritans that Presbyterians might get a foothold in New England as well as to establish Puritan orthodoxy or Congregationalism.

Reverend Richard Baxter (1615-1691) is mostly remembered for his influence and written works that inspired the Puritans and later Christians. Baxter's personal motivation was always the reconciliation between Anglicans [Church of England] and the Puritans.

New England Puritan Church Divines sought his advice on baptism and church membership frequently. No less than twenty letters from John Eliot, Increase Mather, and others are listed in the *Calendar of the Correspondence of Richard Baxter, Volumes I and II, 1638-1696* (Kebble and Nuttall, Clarendon Press, 1991).

Oddly, the 1662 Synod on the halfway covenant set standards for membership that were the same as those standards in Old England as well as other Calvinist Churches in Europe (Holland, Switzerland, Germany). That is, a "membership required a profession of faith in Jesus Christ and an outwardly godly life." [60]

The Synod worded the standards but the results were the same:

"Church members who were admitted in minority, understanding the Doctrine of Faith, and publickly professing their assent thereof; not scandalous in life, and solemnly owning the Covenant before the Church, wherein they give up themselves and their children to the Lord, and subject themselves to the Government of Christ in the Church, their children are to be baptized." [61]

Fundamentally, the Synod of 1662 did not address the REAL issue of the conversion of faithless members of the Puritan society [New England] or even the world at large. Instead, the Synod addressed what it believed to be the critical problem: the baptism and partial [halfway] membership of children, born to the Visible Saints. The children, second and third generation, were those who had not received "saving Grace."

While the halfway covenant may have permitted the baptism of children thus allowing a certain inclusion in the "Holy Commonwealth," it was the issue of allowing communion that was the real evidence of purity with the church.

Even before the Synod of 1662, there was a significant disagreement and application among the Church Divines about communion.

Reverend Solomon Stoddard was the most vocal opponent of the Synod's action since he believed that those who were baptized also therefore were qualified for communion.

A Preparation to the Receiving of Christ's Body and Blood: Directing the weake Christians How They May Worthily Receive the Same by William Bradshaw in 1630 said to adults [children were not to receive communion]:

"The consideration here of not emborden you to be the less careful of the former duties, but rather to make more conference of them. For howsoever those who receive this Sacrament unworthily do not so eat and drink their own damnation, that there is no means or hope of mercy left unto them being fallen into this sin, and though these temporal judgments which God inflicts as signs and tokens, that therein they eat and drink their own damnation." [62]

Bradshaw continues to explain that the bread of the bread of communion represents "those pains he endured in soule and body for our salvation, especially upon the Cross. (1 Cor. 11.24)" [63]

Those admitted to the Communion Table were those "having been baptized, continue in the true profession of Faith and Repentance. (1 Cor 11.27, 28, 29)" [64]

Reverend Increase Mather, son of Richard Mather and a respected Divine in his own right, was well-satisfied with the state of the Puritan church of his father. He was opposed to the halfway covenant but once he realized that church purity was possible with the halfway covenant, he dropped his opposition.

In contrast, Reverend John Allin had volunteered to defend the new doctrine against the conservative critics like Increase Mather. However, Allin's congregation in Dedham refused to allow those eligible for halfway covenant to become members of the Church. The old congregation could not compromise what was perceived as a challenge to "purity" of the church.

In recognition of what he believed New England was losing [by the Synod of 1662], Reverend Samuel Danforth of the Roxbury church said, "New Englanders must stop their drift toward becoming spectators rather than auditors." [65]

Delbanco continues with the observation that Danforth [and Charles Chauncy] believed that the religious leadership had slipped into obsessive pragmatism at the cost of squandering the spirit.

Morgan, in *Visible Saints*, claims that "the halfway covenant, while wholly insufficient as a recognition of the Church's relationship to the world, was probably the most satisfactory way of reconciling the Puritans' conflicting commitments to infant baptism and to a church composed exclusively of saints." [66]

The father of Increase Mather, Reverend Richard Mather, stated his opinion as early as 1651 that "the children of Church members submitting themselves to the Discipline of Christ in the Church, by an act of their own, when as other members, and to have their Infants baptized, but themselves not to be received to the Lord's Table, nor to voting in the Church, till the manifestation of Faith and Repentence, they shall approve themselves to be fit for the same." [67]

Reverend Cotton Mather, as the "last" Puritan, did not embrace the value of the halfway covenant and suggested that the more liberal Brattle Street Church's *Manifesto* allowed any child baptism and communion, would "utterly subvert our Churches." [68]

But as hard as the conservative element of the New England Puritans tried, the halfway covenant was a lost cause by 1690.

Membership in churches had not increased as one might expect of the more liberal halfway covenant.

The focus of this book is primarily on the First Church of Roxbury during the tenure of Thomas Weld, John Eliot, Nathaniel Walter, and Samuel Danforth. The addition of communicants has been established by Robert G. Pope in *The Half-Way Covenant:* [69]

New Communicants

1640-49	1650-59	1660-69	1670-79
7.8	4.8	4.4	5.1

"In the years 1680-1690, the percentage of New Communicants who had not owned the Covenant in Roxbury was 37 per cent in comparison to Charlestown, 88 per cent, Third Church, Boston, 62.5 per cent, and Dorchester, 63 per cent." [70]

Further, there is evidence about the preponderance of women in the Roxbury Church. The women of the church had a consistently higher level of participation both as halfway members as well as full communicants. Males were six per cent less than the women as new communicants. [30% to 36% in 1660-1669, Pope above]

One can observe that during the availability of the halfway covenant to improve the likelihood of full membership and attendance, the Roxbury Church actually experienced a decline in new communicants. It was not pointed out by Pope whether the numbers represented children under the age of twenty-one who had had a conversion experience or not. But the reported period 1660-1669 used by Pope was a stable growth period for Roxbury including the toleration of other denominations. Toleration of other denominations was not a threat to the Roxbury church's membership.

Perry Miller, a respected and profound interpreter of the "Puritan Mind," reasoned [the] "Puritans were a dynamic intellectual force that constantly adapted to keep pace with the rapidly shifting social conditions and cultural climate in the Seventeen Century." [71] The decline of the Puritans speaks otherwise. Puritans did not keep pace with the social conditions in their Commonwealth nor the world about them. Further, and more importantly, they did not understand that their children and grandchildren were not [nor could be] copies of themselves.

In the First Church of Roxbury, Massachusetts, those entering full communion dropped to its lowest point in 1683 (one person) but rebounded in 1685 (16 women, 23 men). [8] Pope does not indicate if the growth in 1685 was from the youth of the church [now twenty-one years of age or older] who had previously had the halfway covenant or were new adults in Roxbury who joined the church.

In 1685, there were 84 adults (40 men and 44 women) who "owned the covenant."

So why did the children and grandchildren abandon the Puritan church? Was it Newtonian enlightenment? [Note: Isaac Newton [1642-1727], noted mathematician, scientist, philosopher, visionary] Was it economic? Was it the severity and unfairness of the Doctrines of the church? Was it lack of communion availability?

The Puritans were outnumbered four to one by the middle of the Seventeenth Century. The non-Puritans had little interest in the severe and austere world of the Puritans. The refuge the Emigrant founders sought quickly was giving way to expansion to the west and south of the Boston area. Control by the Puritans was challenged by geographic spread as well as the social diversity of its inhabitants. The desire by the second and third generations for comfort resulted in a trend toward materialism and profit. Society as a whole reshaped the values of the Commonwealth rather than vice versa.

The second and third generation inhabitants were indifferent to the place of the Puritan church and quickly incorporated into their thinking the move to a more modern society. It is suggested that the halfway covenant was not enough to preserve the original spirit of Puritan theology let alone the theocracy in the Massachusetts Bay Colony.

It has been advanced by some that the furor by Cotton Mather and other witch-hunting clergy was a last breath if not the death of the Puritan grasp of the Massachusetts Bay Colony.

Yet others believe that the real end of the Puritan control occurred when the British Crown revoked the Massachusetts Bay Chapter in 1684 that resulted in the rewriting of the Massachusetts charter in 1691 removing "religion" as a requirement for voting.

It is most likely that all reasons are strong enough to cause the declination of the Puritans. But the overriding thought is that change would have happened much slower if the second and third generation children and grandchildren had not been predisposed psychologically for change. This issue will be discussed in Chapter Fourteen.

CHAPTER FIVE

PURITAN SINS AND BIBLE-BASED LAWS

The Puritans endeavored to apply nothing but the pure biblical standards mainly from the Old Testament to every church polity and every other aspect of life.

The expectation of the Emigrant founders was that a society made up of visible saints would not require any special system of law for the Colony. After all, they assumed, there was the law of England on which to rely if necessary. The Puritans have oft times been cast as "separatists" who wanted nothing to do with things or practices of England. One must remember, though, that the emigrants named their New England towns after the towns from which they came, named the counties after their English counties, and ordered goods and dress from England. Even their military was based on organizational patterns of Old England. It is no surprise, then, that the first ten years of the Massachusetts Bay Colony relied almost entirely upon the Common Laws of England.

However, the Puritan society found that it had, like all societies and cultures, to deal with other issues in addition to "sin laws."

The solution began surfacing in March 1635 with an order decided in the General Court about the number of times a year it would meet and for what purpose. October was designated the month for the development of laws and other occasions.

By 1636, the General Court nominated the Governor, Deputy Governor, and six other aristocrats including the Reverends

John Cotton and Thomas Shepard to draft laws agreeable to the word of God which "may be the Fundamentals of this Commonwealth." It was established that in the meantime, when no law existed, the Courts would hear and determine all causes according to the law of God as they can.

The draft laws were copied and distributed in 1639 to Boston, Roxbury, and Charlestown with the expectation that the elders of the church and the *freemen* [only] would consider them.

John Winthrop, in late 1639, cited that both John Cotton and Nathaniel Ward framed a model of laws for consideration by the General Court. John Cotton's draft was rejected [the reason (s) not given] and Nathaniel Ward's version known as the *Body of Liberties* was adopted in 1641. [Note: the full version of Ward's *Body of Liberties* is included in the Appendix of this book.]

While the law of God was the source for penalties for "acts against God," the Colony created several layers of court jurisdictions. In 1639, the General Court established the County Court system that continues to be in existence today. "The jurisdiction of the County Courts extended to all causes, civil and criminal, except cases of divorce and crimes the punishment whereof extended to life, limb, or banishment [from the Colony]." [72]

The Military Court, established in 1634, handled crimes against the Colony or inhabitants in the event of offensive or defensive wars separately from other Court jurisdictions. It could confine or imprison any who were judged as enemies of the Commonwealth, and "put to death such as would not come under command or restraint as they should require." [73]

Selectmen, elected by residents of each town to attend the General Court as representatives [like a Legislature], were eventually granted responsibility to try civil cases within and/or against the towns. The Selectmen could not impose a prison sentence but could remit the desire for such a sentence to the Court Magistrate.

An additional layer of court jurisdiction was at the town clerk level. This person, who was elected by the town, had the responsibility to "grant summons, and attachments in civil actions, summon witnesses, grant replevins, and to take bonds with sufficient security to the party to prosecute suits." [74]

In the early days of the Massachusetts Bay Colony, there was "no class of trained attorneys who devoted their time to the practice of law." [75] Those citizens who were a party to a controversy needing litigation spoke for themselves without a lawyer. However, an "advocate" could speak on behalf of a person who needed a spokesperson, but could not be paid.

By 1663, advocates and trained attorneys were commonplace in the Colony. However, the General Court excluded all usual and common attorneys from seats as deputies in the General Court [conflict of interest recognized.]

Some early settlers, such as John Johnson, Roxbury, acted as an "attorney." For example, Johnson appeared before the General Court on behalf of Katherine Sumpter of Lambeth, England. Today his duties would be no more than being a representative of an estate or a power of attorney. Johnson had no documented legal qualifications but he could read and write and was able to prepare documents for the courts of the Massachusetts Bay Colony as well as the English Courts. [76]

There was an interesting mingling of church and state inasmuch as there was no portion of the church that was exempt from civil jurisdiction, and no governmental power that escaped the influence of church doctrine and discipline.

The colonial laws begun in 1641 by Nathaniel Ward continued until the Crown of England revoked the Massachusetts charter in 1684.

Erikson, in *Wayward Puritans,* said about [the Puritan] society,

> "Human behavior can vary over an enormous range, but each community draws a symbolic set of parentheses around a certain segment of that range and limits its activities within that narrow range. These parentheses, so to speak, are the moral boundaries of that society." [77]

In fact, the Puritans did exactly as Erikson suggests: reaffirmed the Puritan society's values by putting the parameters around what was, in their eyes, acceptable and what was not.

The Massachusetts Bay Colony was democratic inasmuch as the freemen who had taken the oath of allegiance to the Colony could be elected or appointed to various civil positions. However, John Winthrop "expected them [the freemen] to stay out of routine government affairs. [78]

Winthrop placed all of his trust in his Magistrates to promote and protect the welfare of the Colony. The citizens of Roxbury, for example, were rebuked in 1639 when they petitioned the General Court to alter a law.

Winthrop responded to the Roxbury group saying, "when the people have chosen men to be their rulers, and to make their laws, and bound themselves by oath to submit thereto, now to combine together in a public petition to have any order repealed, which is not repugnant to the law of God, savors of resisting an *ordinance of God.*" [79] [emphasis added]

But the Puritan laws that established the boundaries or responsibilities of the governance of the Colony also empowered the town officers to inquire into the personal moral and business ethics of individual adults *and their children.*

The 1641 *Body of Liberty Laws* imposed a narrowness of a conservative view by Puritan leaders. Even in 1647, for example, a man of twenty-four had no more rights than a child, yet children and young adults alike did have the rights of protection, inheritance, and marriage.

It was sinful to accumulate wealth in the Massachusetts Bay Colony. Yet in 1653, John Glover's inventory of his estate at the time of his death, was valued at 1604 pounds. This sum was considered to be an extraordinary sum of value. Most of Glover's estate included almost 400 pounds in the value of his home and land, 500 pounds in money he had loaned to sixteen people, with the rest of the value of the estate in personal and farming items.

Puritan civil law did not supercede the responsibility to the family of the head of household. In fact, the Puritans acknowledged this in suggesting that "the root whence church and commonwealth cometh is in the family."

Some of the uncommon and unusual laws are cited below:

All residents of a town were required by law to attend the town church.

The law provided that the judges could enjoin marriage, fine, or order corporal punishment as they saw fit.

Reputed fathers of an illegitimate child had to pay for its support and education.

Work was prohibited by law on the Sabbath and even held a master responsible for the attendance at church of his servants.

Required parents to provide for their children because they were unable to provide for themselves, or be fined.

Parents had to see that their children were instructed in some honest lawful calling, labor or employment.

Parents were required by law to teach their children and apprentices to read.

Mary Drury deserted her husband on the pretence that he was impotent, but she failed to convince the court and was required to pay a fine of five pounds.

An emigrant whose husband or wife was left behind [such as in England], the Massachusetts law required the person in Massachusetts to take the next ship back.

Idleness and neglect of duty could result in one being sentenced to the house of correction and pay a fine.

Death was required for a disobedient and rebellious child. [Note: 16. (from: *An Abstract of the Laws of New England as They are Now Established*, printed in London, 1641 by John Cotton and reproduced in *Puritan Political Ideas* by Edmund S. Morgan, (Indianapolis: Bobbs-Merrill, 1965) 178-203.) Rebellious children, whether they continue in riot or drunkenness, after due correction from their parents, or whether they curse or smite their parents, [are] to be put to death.[Note: There were no children put to death in Suffolk or Middlesex Counties under this Puritan statute.]

The court punished young men for not observing the requirement of obtaining "liberty" from a maiden's parents before dating or becoming affectionate.

The law required that all single persons were to live in a family, not alone.

Gracefulness in expression when interpreting the Bible was a sin that could result in admonishment or a fine.

George F. Dow in his *Every Day Life in the Massachusetts Bay Colony,* provided a comparative chart [listed below] that established in 1643, one person in sixty persons was a criminal, whereas in 1915, one person in six hundred persons was a criminal. In other words, there was ten percent more crime in 1643 per capita than in 1915. [Note: this variant may be due to substantial changes from 1643 to 1915 in what was described as a crime and how it was punished.]

Crimes	1643	1915
Murder, Manslaughter, Assault	0	12
Arson	0	7
Robbery, Breaking & Entering	8	176
Assault of Various Kinds	10	86
Drunkenness	7	70
Illegal Sale of Liquor	0	74
Sexual Crimes, Bastardy, Prostitution	6	71
Living from Wife	14	0
Non-Support, Desertion	0	48
Profanity, Evil Speeches	13	2
Extortion, Oppression	7	5
Idle & Disorderly	3	22
Slander & Libel	1	3
Forgery	0	3
Lying & Perjury	2	0
Breaking the Sabbath	5	1
Misc (Oxen in Field, Cruelty to Animals, Delinquency, etc.)	0	39
Total	101	607

Punishment existed for such mundane things as eavesdropping, scolding, neglect of work, meddling, delivering haughty speeches, profane dancing, killing, making love without the congregation's consent, 'uncharitableness' to a poor man in distress, bad grinding at a mill, carelessness in dealing with fire, drinking, tobacco, playing cards, selling strong liquor by the glass, pulling hair, and pushing one's wife.

Practically from the beginning of the Colony, embezzlement, smuggling, and even election fraud were committed. Some of these crimes fell into the 1641 statutory offences while others were apparently tried in court without legislative authority.

Long-term imprisonment was rarely used as a penalty when whipping, fines, and shaming would be sufficient. The reason for the lack of imprisonment was it would cost the towns, the family would be without support, and men [almost exclusively] if in prison were idle when the town needed manpower the most.

Burglars and those who committed break-ins were branded with a "B." The use of an "A" [for Adultery] made famous in Hawthorne's *Scarlet Letter* does not occur in the Massachusetts Bay Colony laws.

The Colony established specific laws and penalties for sexual crimes. It was important to the Massachusetts Bay Colony to foster the virtue of the colonial plantation because it was believed that sins, such as fornication and adultery for example, would bring down the wrath of God on the Colony for not promoting virtuous lives. Further, the civil and church authorities believed that they needed to control their labor sources and their children. Premarital sex and sexual activity between unmarried persons was not only sinful but a threat to the labor force and the Colony in general.

Punishment, even for minor offenses, was always for the effect it had on others in addition to the offender.

The General Synod of 1679, alarmed by the perceived sinfulness of the Colonists, considered two questions: [81]

1. *What are the Evils that have provoked the lord to bring his Judgments on New England? And,*

2. *What is to be done that so those Evil ways be Reformed?*

The answers are plentiful. From the 1679 Synod, they are:

- Great and visible decay of the power of Godliness amongst many Professors [those who profess Godliness] in these Churches

- Pride that doth abound in New England testifies against us

- Refusing to be subject to Order according to divine appointment

- Contention

- Pride in Apparel...especially that of the *poorer sort of people* [emphasis added]

- Name of God hath been polluted and profaned amongst us

- Slothfulness and sleepiness in Church instead of attention and intention

- Sabbath-breaking [not attending Church]

- Family Government is amiss [not praying twice a day together, children and servants not under control of the Master-Father, children being indulged by the parents]

- Inordinate passions [sinful heats and hatreds, backbiting, hearing and telling of tales]

- Much intemperance [sinful drinking]

- Heinous breaches of the Seventh Commandment (Adultery) [laying out of hair, borders of lace, naked necks and arms, naked breasts, mixed dancing, light behavior and expressions, sinful company with light and vain people, gambling, idleness]

- Inordinate affection to the world [desire for land and worldly accommodations, forsaking Churches to live like Heathens, farms and merchandising preferred before things of God]

The Synod was almost prophetic in stating, "In this respect, the Interest of New England *seemeth to be changed.*" [82] [emphasis added]

The Synod of 1679 must not have had much effect, because even as late as 1687, Samuel Sewell indicated in his *Diary* that Charleston feared that the English Maypole that included "dance, drinking, and frolicking had sexual connotations." [83] [with the Maypole representing the male phallus.]

Of course there were capital crimes such as murder. Again in the Sewall *Diary,* "Elisabeth Emerson of Havarill and a Negro woman were executed for murdering their Infant Children." [84] And later that year [1691] "Elisabeth Clements was tried and hanged for murdering her two female bastard children." [85]

By 1684, poor Hannah Goffe of Roxbury was not whipped or fined for her offenses. Instead, according to *Roxbury Land and Church Records, A Report of the Record Commissioners of Boston,* Hannah was excommunicated from the Roxbury Church for "three great scandalous sins: 1. wicked fornication.   2. baudery [bawdery...probably meaning prostitute or house of prostitution but could also mean filthy language] and, 3. contumasy [meaning open defiance of authority for refusing to come to church."] [86]

George Car's wife was imprisoned for "being with child by another man" in 1685 according to Sewell. [87] Also in 1685, "An Indian was branded in Court and had a piece of his ear cut off for Burglary." [88]

Isaac Gross was bound over to the Suffolk County Court to answer for his "conveying and carrying away of Mary Mirack, Servant to Mr. Anthony Stoddard from her relations and from the cognizance of the law she being with childe by Fornicacion and calling of her his wife upon his journey all which hee [sic] was convict of by his own confession." [89]

And, Margaret Preist was bound over to the Court to answer for her "committing of Fornication of which she was convict [ed] in Court by her own confession and brought in her bastard childe in her armes [sic] charging Iosias Rose to bee the Father of it." [90] She was whipped with fifteen stripes and had to pay a five pound fine to the County and fees of the Court.

Thomas Sargeant was examined by the Harvard College on June 15, 1674 for speaking "blasphemous words" concerning the H.G. [Holy Ghost] according to the *Diary of Samuel Sewell* (Wish edition). Not only was Sargeant whipped before all the scholars, he was suspended from taking his Bachelors degree, and had to sit alone and naked in the Hall at mealtime. Punishment in the Puritan era seldom fit the crime!

A servant named Silvanus Warro was convicted for stealing money from his master, Deacon William Parks of Roxbury, Massachusetts by using a false key to Parks' box. The Court sentenced him to pay twenty pounds in money to William Parks and be whipped with twenty stripes. Warro, in the same sentencing, was ordered to pay "two shillings six pence per week for a bastard child's maintenance to save the town of Roxbury harmless from the charge of that child and in case of failure therein he the saide Silvanus is to be sold to the Effect abovesaid...." [91] [In 1668, Warro, a Negro slave, had been punished for running away with William Parks' horse.]

The Suffolk County Court convicted Joseph Pollard for breaking open the dwelling house of Samuel Bill in the night and stealing from him seventeen pounds, fifteen shillings. He was "sentenced to be branded in the forehead with the Letter "B" and to pay unto Samuel Bill thirty-five pounds ten shillings money being the remainder of treble damages according to Law." [92]

These penalties for murder and burglary did not have any effect on reducing such violations in the next decades.

On February 13, 1674-75, "A Scotchman and Frenchman killed their master, knocking him in the head as he was taking Tobacko. They were taken by hew and cry and condemned: hanged." [93]

Bestiality was a problem for Benjamin Gourd, age seventeen, of Roxbury, who admitted having sex with a mare. He had "lived in this sin" [performing this sin] for a year. He was hanged and the mare was killed prior to Gourd's own hanging so he could see the mare killed.

In the cases of bestiality and human sexual intercourse, neither the trials nor the penalties had much effect upon reducing sexual crimes in the Colony.

In *Sex and Sexuality in Early America,* Else L. Hambleton indicated that "those cited for fornication in Essex County, Massachusetts represented only four unmarried and married women in 1641-45 where as in 1676-80, the count was sixty-six women who were cited for illegal fornication." [94]

It has been suggested that with approximately thirty-three per cent of the births occurring before the ninth month of marriage, women and men of the early 1700s were exercising more sexual freedom than every before in the Colony. Likewise, others offer that there was a decrease in parental authority over the behaviors of children by the late 1600s. This author believes that perhaps moral judgments relaxed as the laws regarding sexual crimes were reduced or ignored. It may be debatable that the second and third generation of Puritans totally rejected the Puritan church. However, it is clear that courtship changed by 1700 allowing more and more freedom and less and less parent, church, or government control.

The extent of "bundling" leading to sinful activities can only be surmised. However, the custom of bundling [two people of the opposite sex sleeping in the same bed yet separated by sewn bed sacks], probably led to diverse ways of intimacy that could have produced sinful activities.

Perhaps the young damsel in the Seventeenth Century story knew what she was doing when it was reported that her mother insisted that she put both legs in a pillowcase that had to be tied around her waist when bundled with her boyfriend. The next morning following a bundled sleepover, her mother asked if she "kept her "limbs" in the bag, to which she replied, "Ma, dear, I only took one out!" [95]

Seventeenth Century children and young adults were naturally curious and creative. The consequences and punishments for sinful activities, however, were very severe.

Laws could not control the disruption to family, labor, and the Colony. And, many of the laws were changed after the Massachusetts Bay charter was withdrawn by the English Royal Crown, resulting in similar, but more liberal laws of England.

Ulrich, in *Good Wives,* reported, "By the end of the Seventeenth Century in New England the authority of the county courts to enforce morality had already begun to slip." [96] Fines, for example, replaced whipping at school, church, and at the whipping posts. Convictions for deviant behaviors were less than in the early Seventeenth Century, and the roles of the Church Elders and Church Divines were greatly reduced by the end of the Century regarding family and personal matters.

Of course the greatest number of legal infractions during the Puritan period were in regard to "sins of the flesh." Other sins and penalties are documented in Chapter Two and also listed in the Capital laws section of the 1641 *Body of Liberties* in the *Appendix*.

CHAPTER SIX

PURITAN CONCEPTS OF DEATH, HEAVEN, AND HELL

Death was an ever-threatening, ever present condition to the Puritans, as it was to most of the world's population. Children were particularly vulnerable to die as infants and young children because of poor health of the mother and of themselves. They were just as vulnerable as were their parents to the fear of dying and going to Hell for eternity.

Nearly one out of every three births in the Massachusetts Bay Colony did not live to see a tenth birthday. Some Puritan families had a worse fate. Magistrate Samuel Sewall and Reverend Cotton Mather each fathered fourteen children with only two Sewall children outliving their father, and Samuel Mather was the only Cotton Mather child to survive his father.

What was the thinking by the Massachusetts Bay Colony Puritans about death of their children? There was a realization that life on earth was only a preface to an eternal existence in either heaven or hell. The devout Puritan understood that those who were not part of the "elect" or "visible saints" would be subjected to immediate and great tormenting by the Devil in hell.

Children, especially under the age of four, were not entitled to salvation. That is, the "non-saved" children would go to hell for eternity. The Puritans, unlike the Roman Catholics, believed in infant damnation. As the issue of death is examined in the context of the negative influence on the attitudes of Puritan children who were concerned about their own salvation, it must be remembered that death was a major Puritan doctrine—an extension of the Calvinist teachings.

Sermons at the Roxbury, Massachusetts Church of Reverend John Eliot, second teacher/pastor there, have not been located nor documented in bibliographic collections. However, some of his sermons to the Indians [he was known as "Apostle to the Indians"] exist. Simply, Eliot's sermon style and topics consisted of:

> "God is power, man was a lost soul, Christ the only savior, heaven or hell, according to man's choice." [97]

According to Ola Winslow, author of *John Eliot: Apostle to the Indians,* Eliot did not say a word about predestination, irresistibility [sic] of grace, or perseverance of the saints to his [Roxbury] congregation nor to the Indians.

To perpetuate the fear of eternal damnation and a life in the fiery pit of Hell, parents, the clergy and schools reminded children that children who died young had led a sinful and evil life, and God ordered them sent to Hell.

School Influence

In the *New England Primer*, first published in 1777 with portions used prior to 1777, there were constant reminders about death, sin, and evil.

For example:

> "You shall rise before the gray headed and honor the presence of an old man, and FEAR your God: I am your Lord." [98] (Leviticus 19:32)

Also in the *New England Primer*, even the definitions for the alphabet were taught with reference to sin, fear, and, death. Selected portions are listed below: [99]

A	In Adam's Fall, we Sinned All
F	The judgment made Felix afraid
K	Proud Korah's men Earth sucked within
L	Lot fled to Zoar, Saw fiery showers on Sodom pour
X	Xerxes did die, and so must I.
Y	While Youth do cheer, death may be near

Further reminders of possible eternal damnation were incorporated in the *New England Primer* by the addition of Reverend John Cotton's *Catechism* (Agreed Upon by the Reverend Assembly of Divines at Westminster).

[Note: Reverend John Cotton, born December 4, 1585, was a graduate of Trinity College in England. Originally, Reverend Cotton was called to the parish Church of Boston, Lincolnshire, England. Later, he followed the many former members of his congregation to New England where he was an active non-conformist. As will be pointed out in later chapters, Rev. John Cotton continued to hold children in less esteem *even* after the Divines voted in 1662 to permit at least a halfway covenant for Church membership for the children and grandchildren of the Emigrant founders.]

The *Catechism* from "*A Survey of the Sum of Church Discipline*," was written by Rev. John Cotton in 1645 and published in 1646. School children were required to memorize the *Catechism* along with another of Rev. John Cotton's writings, *Spiritual Milk For Babes Drawn Out of the Breasts of both Testaments for their Souls Nourishment.* Both the *Catechism* and the *Spiritual Milk for Babes*, [listed in the Appendix], while considered to be important reading and spiritual documents, may have actually contributed to the hopelessness of the children and grandchildren of the Emigrant founders of the Massachusetts Bay Colony. The entire *Catechism* is included in the Appendices to provide the reader an example of the overwhelming influences, albeit negative and hopeless, the Church provided for children.

Some illustrative examples from Reverend John Cotton's *Catechism* [100] pertaining to this chapter are below:

> Q. What special act of providence did God exercise towards man in the estate wherein he was created?

> A. When God had created man, he entered into a covenant of life with him upon condition of perfect obedience, forbidding him to eat of the tree of knowledge of good and evil, upon *pain of death.* [Emphasis added]

And,

> Q. What does every sin deserve?

> A. Every sin deserves God's <u>wrath and curse,</u> both in this life, and that which is to come. [Emphasis added]

Spiritual Milk for Babes by Reverend John Cotton (see Appendices) continues the fearful language to which Puritan children were subjected. When asked, "Are you then born a sinner?" The response that **had** to be given was "I was conceived in sin, and born in iniquity." Even though children were most likely sinless, they were reminded that Adam's sin "imputed them and that a corrupt nature dwelt in them. Children were considered to be corrupt and empty of grace, "bent into sin, only unto sin, and that continually." [101]

The subject of "sin" is discussed at length in a preceding chapter, but Reverend John Cotton never gave up on his notion of a Christian theocracy, reminding children that all men were sinners, and that the wages of sin were death and damnation.

The continual references by Cotton and other Divines about wrath, pain, misery, grief, pain of death, hatred coupled with the reminder that "no mere man since the fall [of Adam] is able in this life perfectly to keep the commandments of God, but daily breaks them in thought, word, and deed" must have been a heavy burden for children. The Puritan children were taught about death as early as age two or three.

But did the Puritan parents love their infant children and grieve over the death of infants? Yes, even in spite of the augmented Calvinist doctrine of original sin as conceived by St. Augustine of the Roman Catholic Church. Most Puritan parents struggled with loving yet grieving for their children.

Samuel Sewall, previously cited as fathering fourteen children, "was grievously stung to find a sweet desirable Son dead," when he returned home following his wife's labor and birth. [102]

For Puritan parents, the stress of adhering to Puritan doctrine of infant damnation as espoused by the clergy versus loving and grieving for their infants as cited in diaries and other family papers is not well documented.

As David E. Stannard in *The Puritan Way of Death*, said, "their [Puritan] sense of individual salvation was beset with agonizing insecurity." [103] The Puritan individuals were fierce in the search for signs, any signs, that they were among the chosen "elect" [Visible Saints]. According to Max Weber in *The Protestant Ethic and Spirit of Capitalism*, Puritans experienced "unprecedented inner loneliness." [104] Stannard establishes that the Puritan child's "actual and anticipated confrontation with death is one of many ways in which to gauge the differences" between children of the Puritan Period in comparison to children of the Twenty-first Century. [105]

Further separating Puritan children from the Puritan Way of the Emigrant founders was the attitude of the Elders that children were riddled with sin and corruption and any chance of redemption or being one of the Elect was not possible. There is very little evidence of Puritan children accepting Jesus Christ as their savior.

However, it cannot be generalized that the "Visible Saints" did not believe in the theology in which the Divines instructed them. Infants and young children were condemned to life eternal in hell regardless of the feelings of the Puritan parents.

Reverend Cotton Mather, grandson of Reverend John Cotton, placed substantial guilt on the Puritan parents by pointing out that "your children are born children of Wrath. 'Tis through you that there is derived unto them the sin which exposes them to infinite Wrath." [106]

Seventeenth Century theologians suggested contempt for death, and in fact, a yearning for it. Thoughts of death totally consumed the Puritan.

Peter Gregg Slater, in his *Children in the New England Mind*, states that "Puritan mourning occurred in a milieu in which hell fire was real. The bereaved had heard about it all their lives and had been highly aware of the threat it posed to their children, not to mention their own souls." [107]

Moreover, Puritan children were told to "think how it will be on a deathbed; to consider the terror of certain separation from, and even betrayal by, parents and loved ones; and to imagine what his well-deserved torments in Hell would be like." [108]

Consider these terrifying words of Reverend Increase Mather, son of Reverend Richard Mather, to the Puritan children,

> "Young men and young Women, O be in earnest for Converting Grace, before it be too late. It is high time for you to look about you, deceive not yourselves with false Conversions (as many young men do to their eternal ruine) or with gifts instead of Grace....Death waits for you. There is now a Mortal and Contagious Disease in many Houses; the sword of the Lord is drawn, and young men fall down apace slain under it; do you not see the Arrows of Death come flying over your heads? Why then, Awake, Awake, and turn to God in Jesus Christ whilst it is called today, and know for certain that if you dy in your sins, you will be the most miserable of any poor Creatures in the bottom of Hell." [109]

Strangely, these words came *sixteen years* after children were granted "halfway covenant" for Church membership.

Reverend Cotton Mather, grandson of the Reverends Richard Mather and John Cotton, commented in seeing the decline in religion since the time of his grandfathers, "religion begat prosperity and the daughter devoured the mother." He never got it right that the reasons for the decline of religion were the lack of respect shown to children and the constant badgering about the "sting of death" among other things.

The New England Primer ended with a warning to the Puritan child,

> "Our days begin with trouble here, our life is but a span; And cruel death is always near, so frail a thing is man. Then sow the seeds of grace whilst young, that when thou com'st to die, Thou may'st sing forth the triumph song, Death where's thy victory." [110]

Heaven

Death was made more palatable to the Puritans by the possibility of entrance into Heaven---a real place of rest, meeting relatives, and waiting in peace for the Second Coming of Christ. Entrance through the Gates of Heaven was based upon the saintly actions of the Puritans.

Heaven to the Puritan was someplace "just above the clouds," and was God's "home." The Old Testament [early Puritans relied almost solely upon the Old Testament instead of the New Testament] was part fact and part fiction. Mythology was an important device used by the Hebrews and early Christian writers to provide the Jews and the Christians stories to guide them to a more godly existence.

The promise of Heaven through salvation as well as predestination [as believed by the Puritans] was a central goal of the Puritans and a constant struggle and preoccupation. The utter terror of not being worthy enough for God's grace was a real and persistent theme for the Puritans and their children.

Heaven represented a beautiful home---God's home---and a lovely life in grounds made of jewels and streets of gold [Isaiah 54:11-12; Revelation 21: 18-21].   Heaven, as the Puritans understood it, was the triumph over the punishment of eternal Hell, because of their goodness.

> "When a man dies on earth, God draws his spirit to Heaven." [Ecclesiastes 12:7]

These were the comfortable words that were important to all Puritans.

Calvinist Puritans did not have the meaning of "Heaven" as the modern World now generally believes. Pope John Paul II, for example, in a July, 1999 sermon, pointed out that the essential characteristics of Heaven [and Hell, and Purgatory] were *states* of being of a spirit or human soul rather than places, as commonly represented in human language.

Heaven to the Puritan was one of the rewards from God for their faith and their works. The issue of "God, the Father," is very complex and presumes that the Puritans thought God was a father-parent figure who controlled their behaviors and that of their children with the promise of Heaven [and the threat of Hell.]

The Puritans feared God so much that they worshipped Him with thanks and praise for "Acts of God" such as earthquakes, fires, floods, drowning, shipwrecks, and the like. Their unworthiness [for Heaven] was lifted up as confessions and pleas for compassion and clemency. It was, as author Andrew Delbanco understood when entitling his book, *A Puritan Ordeal*--- it WAS an ordeal and had the meaning a period of time gone wrong.

What became obvious to the second and third generation children and grandchildren of the Emigrant Founders was that even the so-called "Elect" were subject to sin and the denial of Heaven.

> Reverend John Norton said, "The Elect then having sinned, the elect must die, if they die in their own persons, Election is frustrate, God is unfaithfull, if they die not at all, God is unjust, the communion is untrue: If elect men die in their own persons, the Gospel is void, if man doth not die the Law is void; they died therefore in the man Christ Jesus, who satisfied Justice as their Surety, and so fulfilled both Law and Gospel." [111]

If the Puritan fathers constantly struggled with a God and a Heaven that was detached from reality, one can begin to understand the fear that the transcendent theology brought to the children and grandchildren of the Emigrants.

Hell

If Heaven was pleasant and desirable yet somewhat vague, Hell to the Puritan, was anything but ambiguous.

> "Hell is a subterranean place distinct from the tombs," wrote Cardinal Bellarmine." [112]

The traditional vision of Hell held by the Puritans was based upon artistic depictions of snakes, tormenting, fire, the Devil, misery, wild beasts, demons, pain, gnashing of teeth, wailing, and endless floating in the area of Hell. The Puritan Divines constantly reminded the Puritans about Satan and Hell.

The word 'Hell' came from the Greek 'Ghenna.' In the Valley of Hinnom, one of the three valleys surrounding Jerusalem, dead bodies of animals, Gentiles, and strangers or travelers to Israel, were placed in a large fire pit that was never extinguished.

In Luke 12:5, Jesus stated:

> "But I will forewarn you whom ye shall fear: Fear Him, which after he hath killed hath power to cast into hell; yea, I say unto you, Fear him."

Jesus was referring to the fact that those people cast into the fire pit in the Valley of Hinnom would never return and would remain dead forever.

Even though the King James translation probably miscast the Greek word 'Tartaros" [one of the three Greek words for Hell] as the Hell (which actually meant 'restrained') where sinners burn up, the Puritans never believed that Hell was a place for being "restrained awaiting judgment."

Reverend Increase Mather in a sermon as late as May, 1678, continued the vigorous barrage against the Puritan children by reminding the youth,

> "Go into secret corners and pleade it with God...If you dy and be not first new Creatures, better you had never been born: you will be left without excuse before the Lord, terrible witnesses shall rise up against you at the last day. Your godly Parents will testifie against you before the Son of God at that day: And the Ministers of Christ will also be called as witnesses again you for your condemnation, if you dy in your sins. As for many of you, I have

treated you privately and personally, I have told you, and I do tell you, and make solemn Protestation before the Lord, that if you dy in a Christless, graceless estate, I will most certainly profess until Jesus Christ at the day of Judgement, Lord, these are the Children, whom I spake often unto thy Name, publickly and privately, and I told them, that if they did not make themselves a new heart, and make sure of an interest in Christ, they should become damned creatures for evermore; and yet they would not repent and believe the Gospel." [113]

Mather not only reminded the children that dying in sin meant going to Hell, but *in the bottom of Hell.*

About at the same time the whole development of the concept of God beginning some four to five thousand years ago is very complex. But it would be safe to say that all cultures in the world developed the idea of a Supreme Being about at the same time. While it is not the purpose of this book to repeat the scholarship on the history of God, it needs to be established that the well-intended early Christian writers and theologians were quick to conceive rewards and punishments [Heaven and Hell] as a way to change or control human behavior.

Puritan children, in particular, were subjected to an early awareness of death and sin, and that death of a sinner meant eternal life in the bowels of Hell.

The Puritan elders believed that:

a. Hearing about the terrors of Hell would scare the children out of false security and shock their conscience.

b. Hearing about Hell would deter the children from sinful ways.

c. The preaching about Hell was helpful to both the godly and the ungodly children.

The Puritan children were reminded by the Puritan Divines what Isaiah said:

"Who among us can dwell with everlasting burnings?"(Isaiah 33:14)

Further Biblical text was offered such as:

"Who can stand before His indignation? And, who can endure the burning of His anger? His wrath is poured out like fire." (Nahum 1:6)

[Note: Roman Catholics believe in Purgatory as a place for the soul to be purified through suffering in order to enter Heaven. The issue of Purgatory is not part of this book inasmuch as the Puritans rejected those things Roman Catholic. Calvinist doctrine established that a person's fate was determined long before death and this was exactly what the Puritans believed. Current Roman Catholic view is that Purgatory is not a place but a condition of existence.]

In all probability, the emotional and psychological effect of the fear of Hell by the Puritan children could be endless. The whole idea of separating from one's loved ones [parents] is a basic fear of all children. Puritan children were never guaranteed a "reunion" with loved ones because the Puritan children were going to experience **eternal** damnation [Hell].

Children were reminded "before the next Sabbath they may not only be taken sick, but taken away." [114] Further, Hell was made quite vivid when reminded that children were in hell, melting in the midst of the blazing heat of God's endless, dreadful wrath. The stoutest man [this is actually a "children's" sermon!] on earth can no more bear hell than a little bird or worm can living in flaming fire." [115]

Fleming makes the point that little distinction is made between sermons for children versus those for adults.

Reverend Thomas Shepard, an early Puritan preacher and one of the founders of Harvard University in 1636, reminded the youth when he wrote:

> "Formal professors and carnal gospelers have a thing like faith, and like sorrow, and like true repentence, and like good desires, but yet they be but pictures; they deceive others and themselves too...most of them that live in the Church shall perish." [116] [emphasis added]

The Reverend Michael Wigglesworth, a sometime minister at Malden, Massachusetts at times when he was not ill, wrote a lengthy ballad called *The Day of Doom* that was published in 1662. [This poem, based on a dream Wigglesworth had while at Harvard College about "Judgment Day," was no comfort to children who in the same year the poem was published received Half-way Covenant for Church membership.

The Day of Doom was a best seller in New England and England second only to the Bible. Critics in the Seventeenth Century right up to the Twenty-first Century have found little literary significance of the poetic style used by Wigglesworth. But it was never intended to be a "style." It was a message in hellfire and brimstone---enough to scare children and adults into repentance.

Present day critics suggest that *The Day of Doom* is distinguished mostly by its cruel doctrine and its portrayal of the horrors of Hell.

Wigglesworth was not the only writer who depicted the case for infant damnation [though finding for children the "easiest room in Hell." (see v. 180-181)] Even though the debate continued for many years within the Calvinist fold, infant damnation was an issue not resolved until well after the close of the Victorian period.

Examples of Wiggleworth's foreboding "debate with the damned souls of New England" are below:

v. 37

"With dismal chains, and strongest reins,
    like Prisoners of Hell,
They're held in place before Christ's face,
    Till He their Doom shall tell.
These void of tears, but fill'd with fears,
    And dreadful expectation
Of endless pains, and scalding flames,
    Stand waiting for Damnation." [117]

And,

v. 199

"The tender Mother will own no other
    of all her numerous brood,
But such as stand at Christ's right hand
    Acquitted through his Blood.
The pious Father had now much rather
    His graceless Son should ly
In Hell with Devils, for all
    His evils burning eternally." [118]

And to ease the pain of parents whose children had died:

v. 25

"Christ's Flock of Lambs there also stands,
    whose Faith was weak, yet true;
All sound believes (Gospel receivers)
    Whose Grace was small, but grew;
And them among an Infant throng
    Of Babes, for whom Christ dy'd;
Whom for his own, by wayes unknown
    To men, he sanctifd'd." [119]

v. 180 and v. 181

"You sinners are, and such a share
    as sinners, may expect;
Such you shall have, for I do save
    None but mine own elect.
Yet to compare your sin with their
    Who lived a longer time,
I do confess yours is much less,
    Though every sin's a crime.

A crime it is; therefore in bliss
    You may not hope to dwell;
But unto you I shall allow
    The easiest room in hell." [120]

And, to pronounce the judgment about to befall the Puritans:

v. 205 and v. 206

"There might you hear them rend and tear
    the air with their outcries;
The hideous noise of their sad voice
    Ascendeth to the skies
They wring their hands, their caitiff-hands,
    And gnash their teeth for terror;
They cry, they roar, for anguish sore,
    And gnaw their tongues for horror.
But get away without delay;
    Christ pities not your cry:
Depart to hell, there you may yell
    And roar eternally." [121]

Wigglesworth not only dramatically depicted the horrible details of God's appearance for Judgment Day, he recited in his prose "something for everyone." That is, he included all types of sin and all types of those who sinned.

It is said that daily devotions in the homes of the Puritans were based upon *The Day of Doom* in the latter part of the Seventeenth Century and well into the Eighteenth Century.

Later, Reverend Cotton Mather provided no more assurances than did Wigglesworth, when he warned the children in 1695, some 26-30 years after the so-called "end" of the Puritan Period, that:

"I must further, and sadly tell you, You are in a fair way to be the Death of your poor Parents, if you will yet give yourselves up, unto the Phrensies of Ungodliness: I tell you, You'll make Them to Dy before their Time: and what are you then, but Wicked Overmuch. Unworthy Creatures; how can you find in your Hearts to shorten the Loves of those, through whom you yourselves have Derived your Lives?...Methinks, I overhear your Parents with weeping Eyes, and bleeding Hearts thus calling upon you, O Unthankful Children, After all that we have done for you, will you kill us by your Obstinate Ungodliness?" [122]

Children and Puritanism by Sanford Fleming firmly establishes that children had an important role in the life of the churches, "but *not as children.*" [emphasis added.] "They had a place in the churches only as sinners who were in momentary danger of damnation." [123]

CHAPTER SEVEN

PURITAN BURIAL

Thomas Lechford, one of New England's early lawyers, observed [for the 1630s and 1640s] "At burials, nothing is read nor any Funeral Sermon made, but all the neighborhood, or a good company of them, come together by [the] tolling of the bell, and carry the dead solemnly to his grave, and there stand by him while he is buried." [124]

This all but silent "service" epitomizes the burial of New England Puritans between 1630 and 1660. Besides their usual somber ways, the Puritans were forbidden to show excessive mourning lest the Indians [and other non-Puritans] see the funeral as a decline of their presence, and their emotionless response to death as an example of their trust in God. Basically, until the late 1650s and early 1660s, funerals followed the same as might be found in Old England for the same time period.

The range of burial preparation was from no coffin to a double coffin; and from no embalming to embalming the body. Also preparation differences could be related to the number of days after death occurred as well as the social rank of the dead person. But most of the deceased were buried between two and four days. In such cases, embalming of the body was not necessary.

Depending upon social and civil rank, elaborate services generally were not provided for the deceased. An exception was the funeral for Governor John Winthrop in 1649 when the Boston Artillery Officers requisitioned one barrel and a half of the country's store of powder from Captain John Johnson from Roxbury, Massachusetts, Surveyor General of the Arms, to acknowledge the Colony's affection for the departed Governor.

By the late 1660s, funerals became more elaborate for the general public to the extent, in fact, that by 1724 laws were passed to limit the extraordinary cost of funerals.

For the first twenty to thirty years of the Massachusetts Bay Colony, funeral sermons were not part of the finality of service for the deceased. In fact, even the placement of a funeral marker was practically unheard of between 1630-1650. The popularity of gravestones came into being during the 1660s.

While prayers or burials by the clergy were largely absent, the head of the household many times said family prayers. Usually, these prayers included confessions, petitions to God, and thanksgiving to God. But always, the prayer vigil if there was one, included reminders to those gathered about their duties to God.

In keeping with the intent of following the clergy from the First Church of Roxbury (Weld, Eliot, Walther, and S. Danforth) included here is a comment by John Eliot about pain, for pain represented illness and illness represented death, and death represented sin:

> [regarding Mary Chase of Roxbury] "she had a paralitick humor [tumor] which fell into her back bone, so that she could not stir her body, but as she was lifted, and filled with great torture, and caused her back to give out of joynt and bunch out; from the beginning to the end of that infirmary she lay four years and a half, and a great part of that time a sad spectakle of

misery; But it pleased God to raise her again and she bore children after it." [125]

John Eliot represented a period of time when funeral sermons were not used, but he clearly was able to translate every illness and every happening in Roxbury to God's will. Eliot was a strong supporter of obtaining medical education for residents of the Massachusetts Bay Colony at Harvard College. [now Harvard University]

Because of "illness" thought to be the result of sin, it was common for the clergy to take on the responsibility of healing the soul and the body. But even the clergy could not provide remedy for physical ailments like smallpox. Cotton Mather, who acted as a physician-minister, believed that inoculation for smallpox was an "interference with God's works" because it was a prevention of evil.

It was not the physicians who published medical advice but the Church Divines. Many of them paid the price of not knowing about transmitting diseases as several died from contact with contagious persons.

The Reverend Samuel Danforth, the fourth Roxbury minister, apparently spoke at the funeral in 1659 of his three children, victims of an epidemic, just before they were carried to the grave. [Note: Sarah Danforth died November 5, 1659; Mary Danforth died November 7, 1659; and Elizabeth Danforth died November 15, 1659. They are buried in the Governor Dudley tomb in the Eliot Burying Ground near Roxbury.]

The changes from literally no funerals in the 1630s and 1640s to elaborate Church funerals in the late 1650s and beyond, can be traced as far back as 1549 when the Crammer Prayer Book outlined an abbreviated service for the dead that included Scripture, Psalms, prayers, celebration of communion, and committal to the ground.

The Church of England [Anglican] Prayer Book was an adaptation of the Catholic Crammer edition. Basically, the Puritans objected to the Church of England funeral service in the prayer book because of its close resemblance to the Catholic Prayer Book service.

The result of the emigration to the Massachusetts Bay Colony by the Puritans was that there were no controls or Ecclesiastical hierarchy to dictate a set funeral service. Instead, the first thirty years of burials by the Puritans did not have funerals as they were known later in the Seventeenth Century. Moreover, the burial, as marriage, was a civil function, not a religious one.

It has been stated by Gordon E. Geddes in *Welcome Joy:*

> "There is no evidence in New England of the English custom which still persisted into the seventeenth century of burying simply the shrouded body with a common coffin owned by the church being used ONLY to transport the body." [126]

The town of Roxbury, like many other villages in the Massachusetts Bay Colony, had an official coffin maker and gravediggers as early as 1673.

The *Diary of Samuel Sewall* is an extremely resourceful document in regard to the change to the more elaborate funeral service [after 1700] but is not part of this book's focus.

It is not definite when liquor became a staple at funerals in the Colony. But Cotton Mather found it necessary in 1713 to chide the Puritans that drunkenness at funerals was to be condemned for dishonoring the deceased.

As said before, Cotton Mather used the funeral service in the late Seventeenth Century and early Eighteenth Century as an opportunity to teach and preach to the funeral attendees. His 1717 funeral sermon for Wait Winthrop who died on September 7, 1717 is an example of his attention to the needs [as he saw it] to the congregation. He preached:

> "I have the Keys of Hades and of Death. They are the words of our ascended savior which now comfort us and ravish us: words worthy of the greatest attention in the world; the attention of all the world... there is a miserable part of the Invisible World... there are Devils... creatures... wicked... dragons... rattle-snakes, and hideous fiends are there companions... Souls [meaning the congregation present] get into good terms with your great savior... be obedient... never weary of well doing before Him. And I now speak a word with a thousand worlds... where you shall never sin no more..."
> 127

In the First Burying Place in Roxbury, now called either the Eustis Street Burying Ground or the Eliot Burying Ground, an above-ground tomb was erected in 1653 by the [Governor] Dudley family but many of the early burials did not have a tomb or a headstone which was consistent with the practices of the early Puritans in New England. In fact, "all of the land in the cemetery south of the engine house was sold or conveyed to the City of Boston between 1725-1872 for road widening." [128] It is believed that the earliest founders of Roxbury were buried [probably without markers] in the south portion sold 110 to 240 years later.

The lack of tombstones or markers for the hundreds buried from Roxbury in the Eliot Burying Ground possibly can be explained in the following ways:

1. The stones used might have been sandstone and eventually crumbled;

2. There never were any markers, or

3. The selling off of the perimeter areas of the burial ground for street widening removed all evidence of the earliest burials.

Whether there were any doubts raised by the children or grandchildren of the Emigrant founders for the lack of grave markers is not known. It is within the realm of possibility that the religious upbringing about death being God's providence was satisfying enough.

Yet, in other ways, the burial practices were significant in regard to the impact upon children. Burials were reminders to the children that an elder, perhaps a "visible saint," had died and gone to Heaven, or in the case of a young person's death, it was an example of a person dying who had "led a sinful, blasphemous, and corrupt life."

It should be said the burying grounds in New England towns were usually a distance from their church or center of town. This practice was exactly the opposite of the practice of burial from whence the Puritans came. For example, burial next to and even inside the church, was the case in England---even between 1630-1670. Some of the children and his first wife (Mary Heath) of Captain John Johnson from Roxbury, but prior to emigration a resident of Ware and Great Amwell, Hertfordshire, England, are buried in the grounds next to the St. Mary the Virgin Church in Ware and John the Baptist Church in Great Amwell. But John Johnson, his second wife Margery, and at least two of his adult children by his first wife are buried in the First Burying Place [Eliot Burying Ground] some distance from the Roxbury Church.

The distance away from the church or meetinghouse as well as the stark, somber, and solemn burial of the Emigrant founders surely added to the terror and fear of death by the children and grandchildren. The separation from deceased loved ones as well as nothing to continue the memory of the deceased added to concerns about how a body might be resurrected, and was frightening to the children.

Children probably had some knowledge of Calvin's statement that God predestined an individual's fate [for Heaven or for Hell]. It was, after all according to Calvin, a matter for the deceased to wait for Judgment Day.

But for children, death and grieving occurred in the midst of their awareness of "hellfire and brimstone." Each death and burial sharpened a child's understanding of his own vulnerability.

Not personally being certain about their own depravity and always being reminded by the Church Divines and their parents about original sin, "Puritan" sin, death, and Hell, the Puritan child was in a heightened state of doubt, grief, and suffering at a time of someone's death or burial.

More likely than not, children during the period of 1630-1660 were forced to go to the edge of the freshly dug grave so they could "experience the fear of death." This act was a reminder to the children that unless they were sinless and had experienced the religious conversion, God would take their life away to Hell.

Puritans were constantly in preparation for death. They believed that the awareness of death improved the quality of their lives as well as their towns. When a person died, the family and community saw it as an opportunity to glorify God for His divine providence.

Puritans readily accepted this [death] as the will of God. The short, somber, and solemn funeral was for the grieving family and not for the dead. [Note: the period preceding the funeral, the 'deathbed ritual,' focused on the dying person's soul and mind.] Whatever prayers were said at the funeral were for the comfort and instruction in living for the survivors of the deceased.

When William Adams died in 1685 in Roxbury, it was reported by Judge Samuel Sewall that a "prayer was said with the company" [probably meaning family and neighbors] "before they went to the grave." [129]

There was a gradual shift from the somber and simple funeral of the 1660s to elaborate and opulent funerals in the 1700s. The shift after the 1660s was from focus on the survivors of a deceased person to centering on the deceased person.

This shift resulted in not only a more elaborate funeral but with added religious significance such as funeral sermons and graveside blessings. By the first quarter of the 1700s, funeral sermons received approval from the general public. This acceptance took one hundred years of development. But for the older Puritan Divines, a funeral sermon was yet one more opportunity to preach about moral decay, repentance, Jesus Christ, and actually about anything pertaining to the

Colony and towns. Many times it was another chance to remind listeners about the wrath of God in the taking of a life away to death.

Increase Mather [1639-1723], for example, used funeral sermons as an opportunity to warn the people of the dread meaning of the loss of leaders. [That he saw as a sign of his own loss of power as well as a sign of God's displeasure with New England]

Reverend Samuel Danforth [1626-1674] of the First Church of Roxbury [he is the last of the series of the four ministers discussed in this book to provide a continuity of thought and practice] gave 'enriched' sermons containing forty to fifty passages of Scripture and rarely left the pulpit without tears.

Additional religious and societal reforms changed the funeral sermon to fit the theological thought of the particular time period. The holdovers for the Twenty-first Century are at least Scripture reading and a eulogy for the deceased.

By 1700, there were several influences that changed attitudes and practices readying death and funerals. These are:

a. the Age of Enlightenment;

b. the Revolution (showing that people could change their lives and situations vs. the Puritan "will of God theory";

c. the change from a stern God full of wrath to a benevolent God full of love; and

d. Evangelism that accepted death as a natural occurrence but belief that God offered choice vs. the Puritan thought of Predestination.

These changes are beyond the scope of this book generally, but they may reflect a strong desire on the part of the second and third generations to change forever the heritage from their forefathers. It is apparent that rejection of the Puritan Way was practically universal and accepted almost immediately except by the Puritan Divines such as John Cotton, Cotton Mather, Increase Mather, and Jonathan Edwards as well as some later ministers.

CHAPTER EIGHT

THE PURSUIT OF TOLERATION;
ROGER WILLIAMS AND ANNE HUTCHINSON;
OPPOSITION

John Johnson of Roxbury was typical of the emigrant founders who would not tolerate religious denominations other than Puritan non-separatist or congregational. He boldly said, "There is no room in Christ's army for tolerationists." [130] Johnson was described as one of the earliest and sturdiest in the Puritan pilgrimage.

From the very beginning of the Massachusetts Bay Colony, the non-separatist Puritans were distinctly intolerant of any religious group different from what they intended to establish in the Colony. After all, it must be remembered that all authority whether civil or religious rested with the Puritan church and its belief that its member were "elected by God." Survival of the Puritan Way was dependent upon total control of the entire Colony, and toleration of any other religious denomination was unacceptable to the civil and church authorities in Massachusetts Bay. Conformity, it was thought, was necessary to bring about the goals of the Puritans—salvation by Jesus Christ for the Colony's sinful souls.

Puritans were strong in their obedience to principles that gave them ultimate power over every aspect in the Colony. These principles were: [131]

   a. belief in absolute truth [literal];

   b. acceptance of a small elite as official interpreter of that truth [church divines];

87

c. effective unity of the powers of the church and state resulting in enforced religious conformity, the punishment of heresy, and the domination of life by the clergy [theocracy];

d. assumption of a fundamental lack of equality between the elect and others [Puritans vs. non-Puritans];

e. retention of political power in the hands of a few by means of a religious qualification [non-Elect could not vote];

f. belief that government was instituted by God to do his will [theocracy]

Overall, the Puritans' lives revolved around religion and the civil support of that religion. It must be stated that the Colony Puritans firmly were in the belief that Moses was God. While there was acceptance of Jesus Christ, the early emigrants could not accept the New Testament as a replacement for the Old Testament.

> "That whosoever would not seek the Lord God of Israel [Moses] should be put to Death, whether man or woman." (2 Chron. 15:13)

Preparation for becoming a 'visible saint' in the Old Testament tradition was central to the Puritan belief. Part of this preparation was adherence to the idea of intolerance. [Note: one of the other cornerstones of the Puritan faith was LOVE, but this concept applied to love for other Puritans elect [visible saints] and not for non-believers or religious groups outside of Puritan.]

With the underlying philosophy of Puritans that was essentially Calvinistic and Augustinian [Puritans did not abandon all things Catholic!], the distinction between the Magistrates and the Church Divines was clear. The Magistrates or civil authorities were not to meddle in any church affairs and the Church Divines were not supposed to influence the 'government.' In reality, there was a blending of authority and influence because the government was required by its own laws and those of God to promote godliness and restrain sinful men. Punishment by the government was required for idolatry, heresy, criticism of the Church Divines, and blasphemy.

If a person committed heresy for example, the Church would investigate and excommunicate the heretic person from the Church. Then the Magistrates [Court] would order penalties ranging from public whippings to mutilation to banishment from the Colony.

By bringing over to the Massachusetts Bay Colony the English aristocracy, there really was no "equality of men." It was in a sense a dictatorship of visible saints who were determined to carry out their belief that it was God's Elect to develop the New Israel or Zion in the Massachusetts Bay. The protection they thought would insure this New Israel was their zeal to regiment the society from error and the banishment of those who did not believe as they did. Somehow this notion of correcting and purifying the Church of England got lost soon after the Puritans arrived in Massachusetts.

The Puritans believed that any dissent against the Puritan religion would detract from their desire to form the perfect Godly society. Accepting toleration by the Puritans would have been its agreement that worshipping God could be different by different people and yet non-threatening to the Puritan society. Any such agreement about this fundamental theological issue was not something the Puritans could accept. The creation of a Utopian, perfect society depended upon conformity and uniformity.

There were challenges to the rigid, religious thinking in the Massachusetts Bay Colony. Nearly all the available literature on toleration speaks about the threat posed by Puritan dissenters and their 'defection' from the Puritan beliefs.

Any personal feelings about tolerating other religious groups were kept private by most inhabitants of the Massachusetts Bay Colony. Challenges, to be discussed later in this chapter, were from people *within* the Puritan church. But challenges also came from outside the Puritan group: Presbyterians, Anabaptists, Antimonians, Independents, Catholics, Quakers, and Anglicans.

The first real challenge came in 1631 upon the arrival of Reverend Roger Williams from England. Prior to his coming to the Colony, he served as a chaplain to a Puritan family in Essex County, the hotbed of Calvinistic Puritanism in England. Williams was a staunch Calvinist and strongly opposed the ecclesiastical organization of the Church of England. It is believed that his close association with Oliver Cromwell, John Winthrop, and Thomas Hooker influenced his complete separation from the Church of England. In fact, he rejected the invitation to be the temporary pastor of a Boston congregation because it had not severed its ties with the English church.

However, his challenge to the Massachusetts Bay Colony authorities had to do with three theories he had:

1. religious toleration;

2. freedom of conscience; and

3. separation of church and state.

It was these three issues that caused Roger Williams to be banished from the Massachusetts Bay Colony.

As is well known by now, Roger Williams left the Colony in 1636 for what is now known as Providence, Rhode Island, where he became friendly with the Narragansett Indians and purchased land from them.   The "government" of the Providence Plantation as it was called, was based upon religious toleration as well as complete separation of church and state.   Every household had a voice in the laws of the land, and an equal share of that land.   In keeping with his principles, he allowed baptism of adults as well as children. He himself was baptized in 1639 and is considered the founder of the Baptist Church.   In his absence from Rhode Island to England, Williams' plan of democracy was shelved by his opponents but in 1654, when he returned to Rhode Island, he was elected president of the Colony or Plantation serving for a period of three years.   However, Williams continued to serve the political life of Providence Colony until his death in 1683.   He did not serve as a minister upon his return from England in 1654.

The Providence Colony became the haven for those dissatisfied with the bigotry present in the Massachusetts Bay Colony.

It was common for the clergy to write opinions as well as "respond" to others' ideas.   Roger Williams was no exception.   He wrote, but originally denied that he did, the *Bloudy* [Bloody] *Tenant* in 1620 and was responded to in 1632 by Reverend John Cotton.   Williams continued throughout his life to challenge the current hierarchy in order to gain democracy and fairness for each individual.

For the rest of Williams' life he struggled as best he could to encourage and provoke the New England clergy and civil governments to advance the freedom of choice. The 1663 Royal Chapter for Rhode Island clearly established Williams' ideas about the liberty he sought twice from King Charles II. Later, as charters were developed for New Jersey and all of Carolina, the charters were patterned after the Williams-influenced Rhode Island charter.

Edwin S. Gaustad, in *Liberty of Conscience,* sums up the contribution of Roger Williams best: "As to the year 2000 and beyond, one cannot anticipate what will happen to the reputation of Roger Williams, how praised or how damned, how distorted or how ignored he might be. For the sake of both the garden of the church and the wilderness of the world, however, the hope remains that he will not again become an exile." [132] Williams died in 1683 having seen many of his ideas about freedom adopted by several colonies.

Some Puritans of the Massachusetts Bay Colony did follow him to the Rhode Island Plantation in the middle to late 1630s. How freedom or liberty of choice affected the second and third generations of the emigrant founders is not readily known. What is known, however, is that there seemed to be little opposition by townsmen to the Royal Charter of 1691 allowing toleration. The period would be approximately at the time the third generation were young adults.

Cotton Mather, who was a last holdout for the Puritans, had a change of heart. "In thinking about New England's purposes, Cotton Mather did not prove to be a conservative yearning only   for   the   good   old   days   of   unchallenged

Congregationalism," according to Robert Middlekauff in *The Mathers*. [133]

Mather, as a keen student of political reality, continued throughout the rest of his life to help make toleration of various religious thought and practice work. This sudden change of heart is surprising because of intoleration by his father, Increase Mather, and his two grandfathers, Richard Mather and John Cotton.

The other public challenge to Puritanism began in 1637 in the Massachusetts Bay Colony, a Colony with little tolerance for dissension against the established religion. Why this challenge is interesting is that it was by a woman, Anne Hutchinson. Women were supposed to be subservient to the men.

Anne Hutchinson's "crime" was to discuss the weekly sermon and the Bible with other women in her home or the home of someone else. Attendance was extraordinary and interest was high, especially following the banishment of Roger Williams from the Massachusetts Colony.

Hutchinson was brought to trial because the home meetings were "disorderly." The actual resolution passed by the General Assembly in 1637 against her was:

> "That though women meet some few together to pray and edify one another, yet such an assembly where sixty or more did meet every week, and one woman took upon her the whole exercise [by resolving questions of doctrine and expounding the Scriptures] was agreed to be disorderly and without rule." [134]

At the trial, Anne Hutchinson was denounced as a heretic which justified her excommunication from the Church and her banishment from the Colony. Tensions were so high among the citizens and Hutchinson's relatives that Captain John Johnson, the Colony's General Surveyor of the Arms, was ordered to store rifles belonging to the Hutchinson men during the trials.

Samuel Eliot Morrison summed up the events of her trial:

> "it was on a small scale a state trials of the sort then common in England, where no legal safeguards were observe the result was a foregone conclusion. Yet the clever and witty woman conducted her case admirably...Anne's unruly member gave her away. She declared, even boasted, of her personal revelations from the Almighty; and that was to confess the worst. For in this the Puritan agreed with historical Christianity, that divine revelation closed, with the Book of Revelation. Convicted out of her own mouth, Anne Hutchinson was sentenced to banishment from Massachusetts Bay as being a woman 'not fit' for our society." [135]

In 1644, Reverend Thomas Weld(e), first minister at the First Church of Roxbury, wrote *The Heresies of Anne Hutchinson and Her Followers* as a Preface to *A Short Story of the Rise, Reign, and Ruin of Antimonians*. In this instructive preface, we can come to understand the rigid, narrow, and mean spiritedness of Weld which probably reflected all of the Puritans' thought.

The following section is very insightful about the attitude of Thomas Weld:

"They also grew, many of them, very loose and **degenerate** in their practices (for these opinions will certainly produce a filthy life by degrees), as no prayer in their families, no Sabbath, insufferable pride, frequent and hideous lying; divers of them being proved guilty, some of five, others of ten gross lies; another falling into a lie, God smote him in the very act, that he dunk down into a deep swoon, and being by hot waters recovered, and coming to himself, said: "Oh God! Thou mightst have struck me dead, as Ananias and Sapphira, for I have maintained a lie." [136]

Further, Weld said, "These things exceedingly amazed their followers (especially such as were led after them in the simplicity of their hearts, as many were), and now they began to see that they were deluded by them. A great while they did not believe that Mistress Hutchinson and some other did not hold such things as they were taxed for. But when themselves heard her **defending her twenty-nine cursed opinions** in Boston church, and there falling into fearful lying, with an impudent forehead in the open assembly, then they believed what before they could not and were ashamed before God and men that ever they were so led aside from the Lord and his truth, and the godly counsel of their faithful ministers, by such an imposter as she was. Now no man could lay more upon them, than they would upon themselves in their acknowledgments." [137]

[Note: Hutchinson's **"Twenty-nine cursed opinions"** are included in the Appendix.]

Anne Hutchinson and her family moved to Portsmouth, Rhode Island, following the banishment from Massachusetts. In 1643, she was killed by a warring group of Indians.

Even though the Puritan males made an example of Anne Hutchinson for her expressions and alleged heresy, challenges to the Puritan religion continued right up to the Royal Charter of 1691 that allowed toleration.

It is not known if the Anne Hutchinson trial and banishment had any particular negative or positive impact upon the second or third generations. It was, like all opinions, regardless of the age of the person, to be kept private since it was "against the law" to criticize the Church Divines. Clearly, though, it has been well established that women in particular could not have an opinion nor the right to express it.

The ability to have toleration for varying religions, while not acceptable to the Puritans, became the absolute cornerstone for Democracy.

Roger Williams and Anne Hutchinson are just now receiving credit for their early role in the advancement of fairness, first amendment-type rights, democracy, and the equal rights of women.

CHAPTER NINE

COLLAPSE OF THE PURITAN PERIOD

The reasons for the decline and demise of the Puritan period are multiple, not singular. Nearly every Twentieth Century author, though, focused on one of the following as the cause of the fall of the Puritans:

- economic turmoil;

- migration;

- religious dissidence;

- prosperity; and

- population imbalance.

Part of the dilemma of historians of early America is the respect some had for Puritans versus other later authors who viewed the collapse as a failed, religious communal experiment that needed to be put to rest before the society's modernization could take place. It is the purpose of this chapter to explore the various reasons that the end of the Puritan period yearned for "deliverance from the hold of ideas that had served their purpose and died." [138]

Besides the psychological impact of Puritan upbringing affecting the children and grandchildren of the Emigrants, little has been written or documented regarding the effect the three Colonial Wars had on the Puritan settlements and the continuation of that society. However, with the beginning of the King Philip's [his Indian name, Metacom, a Pokanoket Native] War of 1665-1676 and the King William War of

97

1689-97, and ending with the Queen Anne War of 1702-1713, the New England Colonies were subjected to great economic hardships and great loss of life. In fact, these three wars in New England were the most costly wars of Colonial America and the all of the wars of the United States of America in terms of human life per population ratios. Other Puritans and Colonists were captured and taken to Montreal, Canada and many of them did not elect to return to New England after the wars. The extent these wars had on the religious foundations in the Massachusetts Bay Colony are not well-documented. However, it is clear that nearly fifty years of successive wars beginning in 1665, psychological and physical insecurities were unleashed that may have shaken the faith of the Puritans. Examination of diaries and narratives, particularly of those Puritan men and women who were in captivity during the various wars, only provides additional support for the notion that the Church Divines who used the captivity information to advance their own religious causes were in support of a society where violence was acceptable.

Regardless, religion was a cornerstone of Puritan life and its society. The Massachusetts Bay Colony had counted on the town churches to hold the society together. But it was not long after the arrival of the Emigrant founders that religious challenges began to upset the order so needed by the Puritans for controlling the Puritan society's effort.

Throughout the first sixty years in the Bay there were sermon after sermon and religious books after religious books regarding the loss of piety among the second and third generation children and grandchildren. Without the zeal, purity, and fear of God, the Puritan Society was doomed to failure. Religious zeal had been replaced by financial prosperity; purity for a more liberal, personal viewpoint; and, fear of God had been superseded by love of the comforts of the people that prosperity brought.

Church growth was dependent upon two factors: conversion of non-Puritans and conversion of the children and grandchildren of the Emigrant founders. Neither of these activities produced sufficient growth, and by the time England withdrew the Massachusetts Bay Chapter in 1684 allowing other church denominations to exist in the Colony, the Puritan churches all but folded. It is believed that other denominations [Baptists, Quakers, Anglicans, Lutheran, Dutch, and even Roman Catholic] were more liberal, did not require a conversion experience for membership, did not require a confession or examination for membership, and most of them baptized children. In short, the Puritan elders no longer could rule New England by a particular point of view.

Rutman, in *Winthrop's Boston*, wrote that emigrants who were "arriving from England [after 1640] tended increasingly to be those whom the repressive policies of Archbishop Laud had merely hardened in their sense of autonomy from clerical [church] control and their already well-developed conceit of themselves as the saving remnant in a wicked and persecuting world." [139]

It is now suggested that this "hardened sense of autonomy from church control" had much to do with the rejection of the Puritan church's doctrines by the second and third generation children and grandchildren of the founders of the Massachusetts Bay Colony.

Furthermore, it is suggested that the result of deaths from the Salem Witch trials of 1692 was a final blow to the Puritan Church Divines' grasp on the last possible hope for control. Increase Mather and Cotton Mather together were at the opposite end of fairness of the trials. That is, they believed that conviction of those supposed "possessed of the devil" should be automatically convicted and hanged. Of the hundred-fifty people awaiting trial, the civil solution was far better than the Puritan-led attack on the accused.

Many of those accused of being possessed were not indicted by the grand jury and some were actually dismissed from court jurisdiction for lack of evidence. Still others were never required to stand trial. The remaining group was pardoned by Sir William Phips, new Governor of the Bay Colony. The furor over the trials and the wrestling of control by the Mathers finally was resolved, but the Church Divines no longer had much influence over the civil affairs of the Colony. Separation of Church and State actually began in the late 1690s. It is a common understanding now that the Mathers [Richard, Increase, and Cotton] ended up being the Colony's worst enemies.

Another factor of the fall of the Puritans was the balance of the population between Puritans and non-Puritans. Most demographic studies show that the Puritans were never more than twenty-five per cent of the total population except at the beginning of emigration from England between 1630 and 1640. As the Massachusetts Bay Colony moved toward a true democracy, the assimilation of the Puritan minority into the later, more secular majority was inevitable. The successes of the beginning years of the Colony were based upon order and control. The Puritans lost both order and control, however haltingly, as soon as there were in the minority.

By 1640, some of the original emigrants and surely many of their children who were now adult, found it to their advantage to move west, south, and north of the Massachusetts Bay Colony's cluster of towns around the Bay. Part of the reason for the migration was that inheritance of estates was limited to Old English standards that permitted a "double portion" going to the oldest son. Complicating the disbursement of estates of deceased Emigrant founders was the number of children [average six] in the family to share the estate. The mathematics is simple: if a deceased person's estate had, say one-hundred acres of land, the oldest son would get fifty acres and the remaining children would receive ten acres. Ten acres would not be sufficient acreage for subsistence. The average estate in 1659 in Roxbury, Massachusetts, for example, was valued at less than two hundred pounds with less than fifty acres of land with a home and outbuildings. Of the sixty residents of Roxbury, only three had estates valued at more than four-hundred pounds.

But perhaps the most significant element of migration was the acquisition of new land and the loss of control and order by the Church Divines in Boston and the rest of the Bay Colony. Study after study of [primarily] primitive cultures found that they were cohesive because they stayed together in a tribe. The Puritans did not stay together and they did not stay cohesive in beliefs and practices.

The economics of land acquisition and sales contributed greatly to the decline of the Puritan society. The Puritan civil government misjudged the effect of trading and buying land by the early emigrants of the Massachusetts Bay Colony. The Colonists' effort originally was to consolidate their holdings and reduce the time spent in traveling to meadows and grazing lands outside of their commonwealth towns. As people moved farther and farther away from neighbors, scrutiny of behavior was not always possible. And, the longer people lived away from the town's influence, the more independent they became in terms of wealth, comfort improvements to their homes, choices of dress, and religious practice.

Sermons, however, that were delivered to the second and third generations of New England (1660-1690) "would dwell on the graciousness of God in making New England into a fruitful land, and a little later would revert to the older wilderness theme that suggested that personal land ownership and wealth were sinful." [140]

The Church Divines were baffled by the rapid changes in the Colony. Social mobility by purchase of land was unheard of in Old England and was incomprehensible in New England where the Puritan ministers had placed so much trust in the commonwealth concept.

By 1674, Reverend Increase Mather continually preached the theme of inferiors [those of the lower and middle class] challenging the superiors [civil government and Church Divines]. Moreover, Mather pointed out that children were "rising up" against their parents...a violation and sin of the Fifth Commandment [Honor Thy Father and Thy Mother]. Increase Mather and other Church Divines mistook ambition as a sign of disobedience. But it is clear that the second and third generation children of the Emigrant founders were rejecting the oppressive social and economic hierarchy that their forefathers had so willingly believed and accepted as necessary to satisfying God's plan for the "New Israel."

As North suggests, "Success was the one thing that the pessimistic jeremiad sermons [prolonged lamentations] of the Church Divines for the second generation simply could not deal with successfully." [141]

Though for some, though, migration as viewed from a distance of nearly three hundred years, meant the sole reason for decline of the Puritan society. Others, however, viewed migration as the continuation of the process of assimilating a divergent population with just as many divergent ideas, thoughts, beliefs, and hopes.

The point is that the Puritan Church Divines believed that they had built the perfect society with God at the head of it. They were unable to keep the societal experiment alive for lack of like-minded, children, grandchildren, and converts of non-Puritans.

Increase Mather, as the Massachusetts Bay Colony's agent in London prior to the New English Charter, compromised on some of the elements of the Charter that greatly diminished the possibility of Colony [civil] support for the Puritan church. It had always been essential for the Puritan civil-church arrangement [the theocracy] to exist because it meant uniformity and conformity of thought and actions based upon common beliefs. This was never to be again. The first English-sponsored Governors of the Massachusetts Bay Colony [Phipps and Stroughton] had some interest in continuing the Colony's support of the churches. But as Francis Bremer said in *The Puritan Experiment,*"[their] terms were short and troubled. Later English governors had no incentive to sustain Puritanism." [142]

While the Colony had a healthy business relationship with England for the supplies needed in the Colony, the Colony's commerce was becoming more self-sufficient. Along with self-sufficiency came wealth. But one must remember that wealth was first considered sinful, and only after 1660 did the Puritans see it as a sign that God approved of the "New Israel" by allowing wealth.

In the first thirty years in the Massachusetts Bay Colony, the homes of the emigrants surrounded the Meetinghouse [Church]. The residents were in close proximity to each other. They had common goals. They believed in the measures necessary to assure the survival and success of the "City Upon a Hill"---the New Jerusalem. In the latter half of the Seventeenth Century, the houses were less around the church and more around the business square. Priorities were changing from a society focused on God to a society focused on business and development.

To a certain extent, there was dissidence in the Colony regarding slavery, religious tolerance, and political liberty, though this dissidence was quickly crushed almost as soon as it appeared [Roger Williams, Anne Hutchinson]. But, it was not dissidence that pushed the Colony toward modernization. Instead, it was the level of prosperity in conjunction with newly found individualism that caused some of the failure of the "Puritan Way."

As the rigid, restrictive religious Colony gave way to the diversity and individualism within the Colony, and the migration outside of the Colony, so were the children and grandchildren of the Emigrant founders freed of the repressive and psychologically brutal standards that caused mental problems so they could experience personal growth.

It is, in fact, the purpose of this book, to focus on what psychological problems were caused by the repressive beliefs and practices in the 1630s to the 1690s, and how overcoming these problems sped up the decline of the Puritan period.

The decline of the influence and control by the Puritans is more complex, and surely more controversial, than other period of history. We have, unfortunately, put Puritanism on a pedestal, removing it from examination as part of a whole society. Historians are now inclined to believe that the end of the Puritan period was a natural phenomenon reflecting the ebb and flow of the American society as it lurched forward as a member of the modern world.

104

CHAPTER TEN

COVENANTS OF WORKS AND GRACE

Reverend John Preston, a revered Calvinist minister and writer said,

> "You must understand that there are two ways or covenants whereby God offereth salvation to men. One is the covenant of works, and that was that righteousness by which Adam had been saved if he stood in his innocency...and therefore now there is another covenant, that is the covenant of Grace, a Boord given us against shipwrack [shipwreck]." [143]

But perhaps the most intriguing statement by Preston was: "Here the Covenant [of Grace] is expressed absolutely and this is proper *only* [emphasis added] to the Elect." [144] [Remember that the Puritans thought they were God's Elect.]

The covenants or agreements between God and people identified in the Old Testament [Adam, Noah, Abraham, Moses, David, Sarah, Solomon, and Josiah] are important concepts in biblical history and were one of the cornerstones of Puritan theology and practice.

In Genesis 2:16-17, God commanded Adam that "You are free to eat from any tree in the garden; but you must not eat from the tree of the knowledge of good and evil, for when you eat of it you will surely die." The covenant or agreement was expected to be with perfect obedience to God, then God granted life.

The covenant with Noah was to never again destroy the world with a flood. God said,

"This is the sign of the covenant making
between me and you and every living creature
with you, a covenant for all generations to come:
I have set my rainbow in the clouds, and it will
be the sign of the covenant between me and the
earth..." (Gen. 9:9-11)

Abraham had a different covenant with God. He was promised the land for himself and his descendants and as a sign of
agreement, circumcision was instituted as an outward sign of
those who were to keep the covenant.

"On that day the Lord made a Covenant with
Abram [Abraham] and said, to your descendants
I give this land, from the river of Egypt to the
great river, the Euphates." (Gen. 15-18)

[Note: The above passage is the focus of the Jews' belief in
their right to Israel---now only a small part of the land
granted to Abraham by God.]

Perhaps the most far-reaching covenant was between God
and David. In Psalm 89:3,

"I have made a covenant with my chosen one
[David], I have sworn to David my servant, I
will establish your line forever and make your
throne firm through all generations."

Psalm 89:3 is extremely important in that when Augustine
worked out in the Fourth Century his theological understanding of the birth of Jesus Christ, it was essential at the
time to make the birth a virgin one in order to establish the
perfection of Jesus. Augustine's rationale was that Jesus had
to be pure of Adam's original sin   [and not from the seed of
Adam]. Furthermore, the New Testament writers, especially

Luke and Matthew, in the Ninth Century, thought it was vital that Jesus be born in Bethlehem where the Kingdom of the Royal House of David was located to assure the "throne" [of David] firm though all generations.

In these ways, Jesus could be believable as free from sin as well as be the savior [as a continuation of David] for "all generations." But all this needs to be a different book by a different author. Fundamentalists, as literalists of the Bible, have a difficult time accepting the fact that hundreds and hundreds of years of transition went into making the Bible.

The Calvinist Puritans also believed in the literal interpretations of the Bible. The Sixteenth and Seventeenth Century theologians based their writings on rigid interpretation from the *Geneva Bible* [1560].

Puritans saw themselves as <u>the</u> covenant people of God. But the covenant people did not always agree or have uniformity. Anne Hutchinson [Chapter Eight] accused her England and later New England ministers of preaching a covenant of works instead of a covenant of grace for one's salvation. The earning or granting of salvation was by the Covenant of Grace that was reserved for the Elect or visible saints. The early Puritans, John Preston and William Ames outlined the issue of a covenant of works. And it was from Preston and Ames, the that Church Divines received their spiritual information and inspiration.

Ames said in *The Works of William Ames,* about works:

> "1. An action of virtue is an operation flowing
>   from a disposition of virtue. [Mat. I, 2:35]
>   A good man out of the good treasure of his
>   heart bringeth forth good things.

2. In the same sense it is called an action or worke that is good, right, laudable, and pleasing to God.

3. Unto such an action there is required first a good efficient or beginning, that is, a will well disposed, and working from true virtue; for good fruits do not grow but out of a good Tree. [Mat. I, 2:33]. Secondly, a good matter or object, that is something commended by God. [Mat. I, 5:9]. In vain they worship me, teaching doctrines which are the Commandments of Men. Thirdly, a good end, that is the glory of God and those things which tend unto his glory. Do all to the glory of God.

4. But the end and the object are often times all one, both in good and evil actions, especially in the intention and election of the will, where they end it felt is the proper object.

5. For although that good intention or intention of well-doing which is general and confused does not make a particular action good, if other conditions be wanting: neither does a special intention of good suffice for it, if the means be evil: as if any intending to bestow any thing on the poor or upon pious uses should to that end take to himself other men's goods: and a good intention with other conditions doth make very much to the constitution of a good action.

6. But there is required to an action truly good, that at least virtually it be referred to God, as the chief end.

7. In the fourth place, also, there is required a form or a good manner which is placed in the agreeing of the action to the revealed will of God.

8. Moreover this will of God doth inform an action of man, as far forth as it is apprehended by reason. Hence the very conscience of man is the subordinate rule of moral actions: for as every action must agree with a right conscience And an erring or doubtful conscience is first to be laid down before a man may do against it; although a lighter sticking of conscience must not anyway put off any action otherwise approved....

And,

17. Hence our good works, whilst we live here, are imperfect and impure in themselves.

18. Hence they are not accepted before God, but in Christ.

19. Hence in the works of the regenerate there is not that respect of merit whereby any reward is obtained by justice...." [145]

Ames added in typical question and answer writing format of the Seventeenth Century:

"Because from virtue proceed good workes; concerning them therefore,

Question 1. What is here to be understood by a worke? Answer: A worke in this place ought not to be distinguished from an action, as it is distinguished by them, who do account those only for good workes, which produce something that is good and profitable unto men; such as are almes, the building and endowing of Temples, Colleges, Hospitals, etc. For Although among men, which are affected with their own commodities, such workes are in a singular manner above others extolled...Again, even when in such works, not the works only, but the actions be truly good: yet they cannot be equaled to some other actions which carry not to great a pomp. (1 Tim.3.1; James 5.20)

Question 4. Concerning the matter of good works, it may be demanded whether it is not lawful for us at our own pleasure to make choice of something, in which to yield honor and obedience until God? Answer: This is expressly forbidden. (Deut. 12.8.32, Num. 5.39, Mat.15.9, Mar 7.7)" [146]

While the examples above are only representative of the advice of William Ames, it is obvious that Ames' interpretations and advice for the Puritan readers were clear, concise, and convincing, yet firm.

Preston was a bit more rational when he pleaded,

"Consider but how it is with yourselves; If a man should do anything for you, you know he may have many other ends, he may do you many a great good turn; yet if you be persuaded this comes not out of love to me, nor of true respect to me, you regard it not whatsoever it be. If it be but a small thing, if it be done out love, you respect it. So it is with God, works that come from faith and love (for those I reckon to be all one) those he respects wondrously. Therefore we should learn to judge aright of our works, it will help us against that position of the Papists, and also against the common opinion of men.

Every man thinks that Alms-deeds, doing good to the poor, and doing glorious things, etc. that these are good works, when as common actions they exclude, as if they were not good works: But it is not so; we may do the greatest works of this nature, and yet they may have no excellency in them at all." [147]

Clearly, Preston was advising that one should be careful not to assume that works alone would guarantee salvation for works *without grace* had "no excellency."

The Puritans, following their reliance on the Old Testament and God's Covenant with Adam, continued for a time, the idea that salvation was dependent upon good works. Good works had everything to do with being saved from Hell. The works had to be visible enough to be believable that the doer of the works had faith. If the person had faith, salvation was close at hand.

Eventually, the covenant of grace became understood as the way to salvation. However, the written and unwritten requirement by the Church Divines and the civil authorities in the Massachusetts Bay Colony calling for social appropriateness to one another did not stop.

Martin Luther and John Calvin considered salvation by grace alone as "the summary of Christian Doctrine." Grace, then, was offered by God as a generous act that included forgiveness or remission of sins.

But grace was for the already 'visible saints.' For a non-believing sinner, grace and salvation could only come to the non-believer if he experienced a conversion to Christ.

Note the hope given to sinners in the following passage from *An Alarm to the Unconverted* by Joseph Alleine [1633-1669]:

> "Turn you at my reproof; behold I will pour out my Spirit unto you. Though of yourselves you can do nothing, yet you may do all through His Spirit enabling you, and He offers assistance to you. God bids you wash and make you clean. You say you are unable, as much as the leopard to wash out his spots. Yes, but the Lord offers to cleanse you; so that if you are filthy still, it is through your own willfulness---God invites you to be made clean, and entreats you to yield to Him. O accept His offers, and let Him do for you, and in you, what you cannot do for yourselves." [148]

As far as children were concerned, any covenant of grace "who by their parents' covenant were 'half saved,' might be saved by education to become wholly saved." [149]

As Edmund Morgan says in *The Puritan Family*, "As extended [by saved parents] to children, however, the promise was not unconditional, for even a believer's children were born ignorant. The covenant did not give them absolute claim to salvation, but it did give them a better chance than other children." [150]

Covenant theology was a system dependent upon total uniformity of thought and interpretation of the Bible. Covenants of works and grace, for example, do not even occur in Scripture. But in order to make others believe that the Bible or God demanded covenants of work and grace, the Puritans were able to bring about uniformity because of their isolation in the Colony and for a short time, were the majority population. Current theologians believe the covenant theology was really a legalism theology of constant measurement, checks and balances on fellow Puritans and non-Puritans, pulse-taking, and constant do good acts in hopes of salvation. Some writers believe that the reasons so many Puritans wrote diaries was so that they could include all of the acts of good they did should anyone question their salvation. The Puritan theology was a theology that required the impossible from people who could never meet its expectations.

Slater in *Children in the New England Mind* sums up the covenant issue perfectly:

> "However, the need for grace, even if it was consistently upheld, created an unbridgeable gap between the Calvinist theory and that of Enlightenment." [151]

CHAPTER ELEVEN

GENEVA BIBLE; PURITAN LITERAL INTERPRETATION ISSUES

The most influential Puritan spiritual book was the *Geneva Bible*. It became known as the "Puritan Bible." It was first translated from Greek and Hebrew into English in 1560. Most Bible scholars credit William Whittingham as the main translator for the *Geneva Bible*.

However, the first Bible in English was that of William Tyndale who translated the New Testament in 1526 before being martyred in 1536. By 1537, the Archbishop Cramner and Secretary Thomas Cromwell undertook an English translation of the Roman Catholic Bible, the *Latin Vulgate* with significant comparisons made to the Tyndale version in the process of translating.

Queen Mary, in 1553, made every attempt to restore the Roman Catholic faith in England that her father, King Henry VIII, eliminated when he formed the Church of England. Queen Mary banned the printing of any English Scriptures.

Without the attempt to restore the Roman Catholic Church in England by Queen Mary, the *Geneva Bible* or any other English translation for that matter, would have been delayed. But her anti-Protestant effort resulted in a number of gifted, English scholars fleeing [then] Catholic England for Geneva, Switzerland. Within two years, the English *Geneva Bible* became a reality.

The *Geneva Bible* was in use for more than seventy-five years and had an immediate and direct effect upon the English-reading public---especially the common people.

Usually, the *Geneva Bible* was published in two parts, Old and New Testaments, so the purchase could be easier.

The main reason the *Geneva Bible* is so important to our understanding of the Puritans is that it had extensive [300,000 words] marginal notes that helped readers, many of whom had limited reading ability, to understand the meaning of the Scriptural passages.

Teresa Toulouse in *The Art of Prophesying* clarified the true connection between Spirit and external forms by commenting that "Calvin insisted on the self-authenticating nature of the Bible. This Calvinist approach replaced the Roman Catholic Church as the interpreter of Scripture." [152]   Calvinists also believed that the Bible [*Geneva*] contained a "clear interpretable truth [a perspicuity] offered to humankind as well as a special spiritual knowledge available to the Elect" [153] [Visible Saints-Puritans].

But the common, religious English people who were so influenced by the marginal notes of the *Geneva Bible* were told by King James I who followed Queen Mary, that ownership of the *Geneva Bible* was a felony. King James I was outraged at various strong marginal notes that reduced the influence of the Monarchy. Further, he believed that the Geneva Bible overall was "seditious and savoring of dangerous and traitorous conceits." [154]   Eventually, King James I introduced the *King James Version* of the Bible that reads quite surprisingly like the Geneva Bible, minus, of course, the helpful marginal notes.

The following passage from Exodus 1:19 is an example of Scripture and marginal note from the *Geneva Bible*:

Note	Scripture
Their disobedience herein was lawful, but their dissembling, evil.	And the midwives answered Pharaoh, Because the Hebrew women are not women of Egypt; for they are vigorous and give birth before the midwife comes to them.

Another example is from Jeremiah 17:11 from the *Geneva Bible*:

Note	Scripture
Because all Kings Hearts and ways are in His hands, he can turn them and dispose them as it pleaseth him, and therefore they need not to fear man, but only obey God.	Feare not for the King of Babel, of whome ye are afraid: be not afraid of him faith [unto] the Lord: for I am with you, to save you, and to deliver you from his hand.

And finally, an example is cited of a Psalm, Psalm 16, and its lengthy marginal note. All of the Psalms in the *Geneva Bible* have <u>extensive</u> marginal notes. Following is Psalm 16 from the *Geneva Bible*; the same Psalm from the *King James Version Bible*; and lastly, the same Psalm from the *New Revised Standard Version Bible* for comparison:

Note	Scripture
He showeth that we cannot call upon God except we trust in him. Though we cannot enrich God yet we must bestow God's gifts to the use of his children. As grief of conscience and miserable destruction. He would neither by outward processing nor in heart nor in mouth consent to their idolatries.	Preserve me, O God; for in thee do I trust.
	O my soul thou hast said unto the Lord. Thou art my Lord: my well-doing extendeth not to thee.
	But to the Saints that in the earth; and to the Excellent: All my delite is in them.
Wherein my portion is measured. God reaches me continually by secret inspiration. The faithful are sure to persevere to the end.	The sorrows of them, that offer to another God, shall be multiplied: their offering of blood will I not offer, neither make mention of their names with my lips.
That is, I rejoice both in body and in soul.	The Lord is the portion of mine inheritance and of my cup; thou shalt maintain my lot.
This is chiefly meant of Christ, by whose resurrection all his members have immortality. Where God favors, there is perfect unto felicity.	The lines are fallen Me in pleasant places: yea, I have a fair heritage.
	I will praise the Lord, who hath given me counsel: my reines teach me in the night.
	I have set the Lord always

before me: for is at my right hand: therefore I shall not slide.

Wherefore mine heart glad and my tongue rejoiceth: my flesh also doeth rest in hope.

For thou wilt not leave my soul in the grave: neither will thou suffer thine holy one to see corruption.

Thou will show me the path of life: in thy presence is the fullness of joy: and at thy right hand there are pleasures for evermore.

Preserve me, O God: for in thee do I put my trust.

O my soul, thou hast said unto the Lord, Thou art my Lord: my goodness extendeth not to thee;

But to the saints that are in earth, and to the excellent, in whom is all my delight.

Their sorrows shall be multiplied that hasten after another God: their drink offerings of blood will I not offer, nor take up their names into my lips.

The Lord is the portion of mine inheritance and of my cup: thou maintainest my lot.

The lines are fallen until me in pleasant places; yea, I have a goodly heritage.

I will bless the Lord, who hath given me counsel: my reins also instruct me in the night seasons.

I have set the Lord always before me: because he is at my right hand, I shall not be moved.

Therefore my heart is glad, and my glory rejoiceth: my flesh also shall rest in hope.

For thou wilt not leave my soul in hell; neither wilt thou suffer thine Holy One to see corruption.

Thou wilt shew me thy path of life: in the presence is fullness of joy; at thy right hand there are pleasures for evermore.

Protect me, O God, for in you I take refuge. I say to the Lord, "You are my Lord: I have no good apart from you."

As for the holy ones in the land, they are the noble, in whom is all my delight.

Those who choose another God multiply their sorrows; their drink offerings of blood I will not pour out or take their names upon my lips.

The Lord is my chosen portion and my cup; you hold my lot.

The boundary lines have fallen for me in pleasant places; I have a goodly heritage.

I bless the Lord who gives me counsel; in the night also my heart instructs me.

I keep the Lord always before me; because he is at my right hand, I shall not be moved.

Therefore my heart is glad, and my soul rejoices; my body also rests secure.

For you do not give me up to She'ol, Or let your faithful one see the Pit.

You show me the path of life. In your presence there is fullness of joy; in your right hand are pleasures forevermore.

King James I believed that the marginal note in the first example suggested disobedience to him, a King. The *Geneva Bible* was definitely the household Bible in Old England and New England. Later versions of the *Geneva Bible* eliminated what was described as "strident tones of Puritan ethics." But the *Geneva Bible* was never the authorized Bible of the Church of England.

The *Geneva Bible* was the Bible brought exclusively to America beginning in 1607 [Jamestown] to well after the emigration that began in 1630 to the Massachusetts Bay Colony. It was the "peoples' bible.

It was this Bible with the marginal notes that gave the Puritans guidance, direction, and focus. [Note: The Book of Common Prayer of the Church of England commonly was found listed in the Wills of the Puritan Emigrants. Obviously, the Puritans did not reject all elements of the Church of England.]

Furthermore, Stout claims in his article, *"Word and Order in Colonial New England,"* once the "people had been indoctrinated in the truths of Holy Writ, it was possible to begin moving to the second, and more ambitious phase of building an ***entire social order according to scriptural blueprint.***" [155]

The marginal notes represented individual and group decisions by the forty-seven Anglican and Puritan translators regarding interpretation. Even though the changes made to the Bible number at least 100,000 changes, the essence of the Scripture has not changed.

It has been viewed that the Puritans, holding onto rigid, literal, religious viewpoints and practices, were major factors in the discouragement in the children and grandchildren of the emigrant founders.

It may not be possible to know if the Puritans first became "Elect" [and to establish a New Israel] then later becoming rigid in the literal Bible interpretation based on the *Geneva Bible* or vice versa. However, in the examination of the first four ministers at the Roxbury, Massachusetts Church, interpretations were void of any changes that occurred in the 70-year history of the four successive ministers. Just as the *Latin Vulgate Bible* would outlast its purpose, it is thought the Puritans, by holding onto their literal Bible interpretations, outlasted their second and third generation children and grandchildren.

An example of change and interpretation, is to remind readers that the 1611 *King James Version Bible* [that replaced the *Geneva Bible*] has undergone three revisions that incorporated 100,000 changes. Furthermore, more than 300 words in the *King James Version Bible* no longer have the same meaning as in 1611. It also must be remembered that the Marginal Notes of the *Geneva Bible* reflected the understanding, bias, and the society and culture of the translators and were not always faithful to the Hebrew and Greek language of the original documents from which the *Geneva Bible* was translated.

While the Puritan jurisprudence and its reliance upon the Bible as its source of the principles of law has been discussed at length in *Chapter Five*, the legal development had to pass Biblical scrutiny. In a theological sense, the Puritans were proponents of the Bible's original intent, and they believe since they were God's Elect, they were justified in placing God's law [as they interpreted it] above all other law.

As Haskins observed:

> "Even when they professed and appear to be following God's word most literally, they were influenced by their English inheritance, intellectual as well as legal, and by pragmatic or expedient considerations growing out of the conditions of settlement, the same kind of eclecticism that was motivated, guided, and made coherent by the distinctive ethic that marked Puritan scholarship generally is clearly apparent in the shaping of Massachusetts law. For all their reverence for the Scriptures, the colonists almost never enacted literal Bible texts as law before those texts had passed a rigorous logical justification."

> The Bible in Massachusetts was an indispensable touchstone, but not the cornerstone of Puritan legal thinking. Central as was its position in Puritan life and thought, it was only one influence among many in a rich cultural heritage which was quickened by the challenge of new problems in a new land." [156]

It is not the rigid adherence to the laws based upon the Bible the Puritans developed in 1641 that could be criticized but the laws that were developed that regulated the place of women, freedom of choice of work, education, religion, marriage partners, personal dress, behavior, and one's ability to achieve one's potential that is questioned.

Dangers of Literal Interpretation of the Bible

Even today there are religious denominations that adhere to absolute, literal interpretations of the Scriptures that seem uncannily like those of the Puritans. The dangers of literal interpretation for children and family are many.

Drawn from Daniels, Greven, Morgan, Underdown, and Spong, the Puritans, like today's Fundamentalists and Pentecostals, interpreted the Bible in the following ways:

1. without having brought any sense of culture, distance [of time], or religious evolution to their understanding, interpretation, and practice or implementation.

2. without any recognition that language or meaning of language changes that could or would affect meaning.

3. with the belief that focus of their interpretation would be also their application [it was common for the Puritans to find reason and justification to meet what they deemed to be the right way to solve a sinful or civil or religious problem.]

4. without an understanding that some of the Scripture was written hundreds of years after the event [there were no witnesses] and reflected what the Roman Catholic Church or the followers of Jesus wanted to have understood.

5. without an understanding of Newtonism and Enlightenment.

The marginal notes, previously cited, not only replaced the need for any interpretation by the Roman Church, they served as a common literary effort that bound all non-Catholic people together. As Harry S. Stout states in his article, *"Word and Order in Colonial New England,"* "The physical linkage of text and commentary on every page gave added weight to the notes and gave them the appearance of a direct extension of scared writ. When we view the contents of these notes we are observing the symbolic universe of popular piety at its most direct and formative level." [157] The commentaries or marginal notes had a significant influence on religious understanding and practice and were considerably more important than some "sermons, devotionals, and spiritual autobiographies." [158]

With the Bible being interpreted by the Puritan Divines as a spiritual experience, the opportunity to understand what was really in the heart and mind of the Puritans was lost after the first generation emigrants.

The Puritan Massachusetts Bay Colony society was, in a sense, a closed society nearly removed from challenges by England in particular, and the world at large. Church Divines such as Richard Mather, Increase Mather, Cotton Mather, and Reverend John Cotton, were the most conservative clergy who defended old views. Because of the thousands and thousands of pages of sermons, books, and diaries, more is known about the Mathers and John Cotton than all of the other clergy in New England. There may be other clergy who held tightly to views like the Mathers and Cotton but their views are not as well known. As the church in New England remained stagnant in the last half of the Seventeenth Century, the society was attempting to move forward. And, the challenges were coming from all sides. Thomas Hobbes, an English political philosopher, "rejected both the authority of

the Catholic Church and the bibliolatry of Protestantism." [159]
He did not believe the Bible was "uniquely inspired." [160] At
the same time, John Locke, a vigorous exponent of free
inquiry and toleration, believed in being rational about the
meaning of Scripture.

Because the Puritans viewed God as an all-knowing and
powerful force in their lives, they believed that their wealth
and successes were a sign that they were not only correct but
Elect. They chose to stamp out anything that might interfere
with their correctness, even when decisions were not
Biblically correct.

Dr. Elliot Johnson in *Expository Hermeneutics: An
Introduction*, believes that "literal interpretation refers to
systems of interpretation when the clear, plain sense of a
word or phrase is understood over against a figurative use,
and a system that views the text as providing the basis of *true
interpretation*." [161] [emphasis added]

The Elliott Johnson system would conclude that even though
we might look at the Bible differently, we believe that
everyone else should find exactly the same answers in the
Bible. The Puritans believed their Scriptural positions were
valid Scriptural teachings. As Toulouse suggested in *The Art
of Prophesying*, "Whether listeners are *Elect* or non-*Elect*,
they are equally commanded to participate in the sharing of
the "milke" of *Elect* preaching." [162]

"No one", according to Larry Chouinard in the *Christian
Standard*, "in the First Century possessed all twenty-seven
books of the New Testament." [163] Chouinard writes,
"Twenty-first Century people dig deeper into the truth as they
seek to guide others to God. One must be aware of
differences between Bible times and our present times." [164]
The Puritans did not keep these differences in mind.

Skilled Biblicists can many times explain the problems of the Bible. The problems or questions about the Bible are not so much related to whether the Bible was written or inspired by God, but more because the Bible was written by men, translated by men, interpreted by men, and used for controlling men. The Puritan obsession with the Bible led them to incorporated aspects of the Jewish faith into their lifestyle as well as their community. Much of their literal interpretation of the Old Testament was not in agreement with the Jewish views nor the actual Jewish implementation or practice. But the main expectation by the Puritans was that the Bible would give them grace, for grace was a necessary ingredient or covenant for salvation of the soul. Preaching, while greatly respected and frequently done, was not argued by the Puritans as the only way to grace. Even Reverend John Cotton argued "there is a mighty power in the Holy Scriptures to supply the faith of God's people." [165]

Unfortunately for non-Puritans, there was no assurance for the receipt of grace from preaching or the Bible. Toulouse commented, "the spirit moves through the *Elect* Preacher, through the words he speaks from the Scripture and from thence into the hearts of *Elect* hearers." [166]

In the Puritan effort to "cleanse" the Church of England of its Popish leanings and its myths and falsehoods, they developed tyrannical practices, myths, and falsehoods of their own.

With the onset of the *Age of Enlightenment*, coupled with the advancing freedoms of choice, work, marriage, education, and religion by 1700, permitted the second, and surely allowed the third generations of the emigrants, to remove themselves from the rigid, repressive, religious environment of the Puritan theocracy.

A fairly recent survey of students at America's largest *evangelical* seminaries revealed that "more than eighty-five per cent of the students did not believe the Bible is totally accurate in terms of faith, history, and secular matters," [167] according to George A. Marsden in his book, *Reforming Fundamentalism.*

Sociologist Jeffery Hadden in 1987, in a study of change of belief asked the following Protestant denominations whether or not the Bible was the inspired and inerrant Word of God. The percent of each of these denominations who responded "No" follows: [168]

Episcopalians	95%
Methodists	87 %
Presbyterians	82 %
American Lutherans	77 %
American Baptists	67 %

We do not have any surveys of how Puritans viewed the inerrancy of the Bible. The Puritans believed that the Scriptures reflected exactly what God was saying. A strong assumption can be made that they did not begin to question the accuracy of the Bible until well after the First Great Awakening. And, we can assume that the Puritan men and women tried hard to be godly and devout in believing the Scriptures as in the *Geneva Bible.*

Lastly, with the recognition that they could not maintain the same zeal for religion and the Bible as did their forefathers, the second and third generation children and grandchildren of the emigrants found it easy to abandon the Puritan Way of their forefathers.

CHAPTER TWELVE

CHILDREN, ADOLESCENTS, AND FAMILIES
IN THE PURITAN SOCIETY

Any examination of a society must include how that society viewed its children and adolescents by the families as well as by the civil and church authorities. Scrutiny of the concept of childhood helps us to understand not only the Puritan period but the successive generations. The Puritan period then becomes an "American" baseline to judge our Western society---recognizing that children have been around since the beginning.

Robert Filmer, a Sixteenth Century political theorist from England, provided tremendous insight by challenging the divine right of the Monarchy as well challenging the whole concept of the relationships of children and parents...especially fathers. But in the end, he concluded that "kings are fathers, and fathers are kings." [169] Filmer, nonetheless, established in the 1500s the concept of responsibility of the "father and even the state to provide food, shelter, and education." [170]

In the Puritan world, the care and treatment [discipline] of children actually was the responsibility of the father. From roughly 1500 to 1660, the child and child-rearing practices were represented by rejection, isolation, flogging, and harsh discipline. While the Puritan family was representative in child treatment, it had the extra dimension of Calvinistic views about the depravation of children, hell, and of salvation. It is not suggested that child-rearing theories were widely accepted world-wide. In reality, the changes in treatment of children first appeared in the early- to mid-Seventeenth Century in England and were eventually partially accepted by New England. The Puritan children never escaped the repressive nature that affected individualism.

Part of the problem of childrearing by the Puritans was that they were always at "war" with sin in hopes that force would provide victory over it. It has been argued that Puritan parents from the higher social class were in receipt of emotional satisfaction from their children and took great pride in the "serious" accomplishments of them. Perhaps the apparent strong emotional bonds and lasting relationships are based more on the fact that the likes of Josselyn, Increase Mather, Cotton Mather, John Cotton and Samuel Sewell wrote diaries whereas parents of the middling and lower classes did not write as many or as much.

Parenting is a good example of hearing or reading about child discipline in the church setting but ignoring Church Divine advice once in the home. Reverend Increase Mather was so concerned about the "sinful indulgence" by parents toward their children that he frequently sermonized on the subject. Of course, Reverend John Cotton wrote a tract called *Duties of Parents to Their Children.* [171] (and, vice versa)

By the Eighteenth Century, childrearing gave way, in spite of the Church Divines, to tolerance, mutual understanding, and affection. It is now believed that these changes occurred because the discipline shifted from the father to the mother. And, there is a possibility that parents were refusing to be as authoritarian as their forefathers.

Various authors from Pollock, Morgan, Demos to Aries, Hoyles, Stone and others came to views about Puritan children that represented opposing concepts yet none of them are necessarily in error. Dependence upon the diaries of children, diaries of parents, and the diaries and sermons of clergy provide some insight into how children were understood, how they were treated, and what they thought.

It has been suggested by Linda Pollock in *Forgotten Children* "they [the child diarists] from evidence contained in their diaries were not repressed, severely disciplined beings." "In fact," she said, "they noted less punishment than the adult diarists which suggests that they were not subjected to a harsh discipline." [172] It is this kind of conclusion by Pollock that is surprisingly insensitive to what we now know about children---they tend to believe that they "deserve" the punishment rendered by their parents. Contrary to Pollock's conclusion, Fischer in *Albion's Seed,* reported that it was common discipline for restless children to be "rolled into a ball, with knees tied under their chins, and batted back and forth across the floor by adults. Sometimes, even the older children took part in this punishment." [173] Another example of Puritan punishment for children who lied or bit the finger of an adult resulted in the children wearing a sign around their necks proclaiming their offenses, "Little Lying Boy, " or "Finger Biting Baby." Many of the adult diaries, moreover, were written to assure future readers that the writers of the diaries had "good works and good grace." The reliability of these adult diaries is somewhat suspect.

The Puritan children are shockingly similar in many respects to all children in the Western world and perhaps the whole world.

Any parental advice [and there was a lot] from the Puritan pulpit likely was treated like some of the sermonizing: polite listening to polite rejection once home.

Yet, Puritan parents seemed resourceful for the most part. Even though parents in the early to late Seventeenth Century were apprehensive and unsure about child-parent relationships, they were clear about religion, values, and work. Like most parents, even in the Twenty-first Century, these parents agonized over whether their children would be self-sufficient, educated, and have good values---and go to heaven.

Parents now and parents in the Puritan period tend to parent as they were parented. And, the children of today will parent as they were parented with minor modifications just as the Puritan parents modified their child-care practices.

However, though the variables of parenting are small, there were factors of Puritan parenting which, when coupled with the Puritan culture, reduced for some the chances of self-worth, personal growth, education, and the obtaining of moral values. As Slater said in *Children in the New England Mind,* "Children thereby served as vehicles for carrying into the future the moral traditions of the past." [174]

The complexity of rearing children in the Puritan period accounts for the disparity of divergent opinions and practices. A few are cited in the following paragraphs.

Even though the death rate in the Massachusetts Bay Colony was approximately one to every three births, the Puritan women, because they married two to three years [at age 23 years] younger than their Old England cousins, had more births in New England. Over all, it was thought by Lockridge in *A New England Town,* that [New England] "had better diet, better housing, and conditions which acted year in and year out to prolong the lives of older persons and to ensure that more infants survived the critical days following birth." [175]

By the mid-Seventeenth Century, the birth rate/death rate was ten to one. New England did not escape the epidemics of measles, dysentery, diphtheria, and smallpox. There were, according to town birth records, gaps of two to four years between births, reflecting deaths from disease rather than, as has been suggested, birth control based upon breastfeeding.

Whereas the Roman Catholics provided baptism and salvation for children, the Puritans viewed the death of a child Hell-bound. Baptism would not have made any difference. "Infants," Calvin believed, "were torn from their mothers' breasts, into eternal death." [176]

Some Puritan clergy, however, did baptize babies and young children but stressed that such baptism did not guarantee salvation from Hell. On the other hand, some churches, like those in Salem, Massachusetts, refused to baptize children of non-members.

Puritan church membership and Puritan church attendance are two different things. Attendance was required of all of those living in the towns in the Massachusetts Bay Colony by law. But church membership was only for those Elect individuals who had a covenant of grace and who were visible saints by public confession of a conversion experience. Rutman suggests, in *Winthrop's Boston*, that "non-members could and probably in some measure, did attend services in the church, though regularity was undoubtedly lack in the great majority and the number absent from any given service, large." [177]

Children of the Elect most assuredly attended church with their parents but they could not be members and they could not receive communion. And in some Massachusetts Bay Colony churches, could not even be baptized.

Government of the church was limited to adult members only. Until the children publicly "professed" before the church and had a Christian conversion experience that they could relate, their importance was negligible.

After all, Calvinist clergy assumed that all infants and children were depraved [because of the Original Sin] from the very beginning of birth. This depraved state was not thought not to be easily overcome. And, in fact, "increased in strength as the individual advanced in years, unless checked by *outside* forces." [178]

Historians now believe that many parents did not always adhere to what the Church Divines had to say about the "depraved state" of children. There are many expressions of pleasure with children and grandchildren in the literature.

Death was a perpetual fear for children because they were exposed to the death of loved ones and friends, and were constantly and consistently reminded that their fate was damnation or that they would be thrown down to Hell for seemingly [now] minor infractions.

According to Laurel Thatcher Ulrich, "some parents dealt with the fragility of life and death through emotional disengagement, a mode which could lead to *indifference if not outright neglect.* " [179] [emphasis added]

Yet even Reverend Cotton Mather commented that "We have taken our children from us; the desire of our eyes taken away in a stroke." This was said as he spoke about the fear of sudden death of an infant or child.

Rather than the somber, tearless, emotionless image of Puritans portrayed by historians and the media, most children and parents mourned the death of loved ones. In fact, Slater suggested that because the "death watch" could extend for many days, the mourning was all but over by the actual occurrence of death or burial. He believed that since the evidence is lacking in regard to emotion at the burial is an indication that mourning took place in the preceding days of death.

While the Puritans had the order of the world worked out (God for the world; World for God; Man for God and vice versa) any possibility of humans being equal during their lifetimes was not in the scheme of things.

Children were taught very early about class rank. Not only did the children understand superiority of men over wives and children, they understood the Gentry class over the lower class; Elect over non-Elect; church member over non-church member; Puritans over Indians, and on and on. Instruction to children about class distinction was all about "God's plan" for social order. Children, of course, within the family were at the bottom of the family social order.

Social rank is clearly one of the trappings of Old England that was brought to the Massachusetts Bay Colony. Whereas the Puritans were quick to discard "Popish" elements of the Church of England, they were not so anxious to do away with the heritage of English social ranking.

Even as "democracy" was discussed and questioned by John Winthrop, John Cotton, and others [primarily from the higher social rank], John Cotton said, "If the people be governors, who shall be governed?" [180] As we have learned previously, the right to challenge a law such as did the Roxbury residents, was not a possibility in the Puritan period. Challenge meant that God had not been kept in the proper perspective. God first. God, as thought by the Puritans, had created the proper social order and expected men to live harmoniously within church, family, and government. Individual freedom in Puritan New England was only possible in government-selected choices of work, church, town membership, and in the case of single people and servants, in what family they should live.

The issue of social order and democracy within the family was clearer than social ranking based upon education, wealth, titles, and position in the colony.

The man/husband was in charge of all who lived in his house: wife, children, other people's children, servants, old parents, non-relative single men and women.

Church Divines tried to discourage the mixing of social rank. For example, a man should not marry his maid; a man should not marry a non-baptized female; a man should not marry a non-church member. Marrying "equals" was the rule in the Puritan period. Further, seating in the Meetinghouse (church) was by social rank with the highest level sitting in front and the common class of servants and farm hands sitting in the back of the church. Likewise, similar distinctions were made at Harvard College where the students were arranged in the catalog, not alphabetically or in recognition of proficiency as students, but according to the *social standing of the families* of which they were members.

Puritan parents were obligated to and responsible for putting their children in the way of God by taking them to church twice on Sundays and having religious instruction three or four times in the home during the week. Parents and children used John Cotton's *Spiritual Milk for Babes Drawn Out of the Breasts of Both Testaments for Their Souls and Nourishment* [in the Appendix] in home religious instructions.

Discipline was an essential element growing up in a Puritan family. The sinful nature of children as thought by Puritan church Divines and accepted by Puritan parents, all but required parents to discipline their children, some harshly. In Cotton Mather's *Help for Distressed Parents,* he advised parents that "children were better whipt, than Damn'd." [181]

Whipping and other forms of physical discipline were utilized to "break the will of the child,"---a Calvinist child-rearing methodology. Samuel Sewall, a Magistrate, whipped his son Joseph *pretty smartly* for throwing a knop of brass and hit his Sister Betty on the forehead so as to make it bleed and swell. "Beatings, indeed seem at that [Puritan] time to have constituted the most essential part of education." [182] Unfortunately, whipping and more severe punishments are still being practiced by some parents, other groups, and, in fact, encouraged by some members of Fundamental and Pentecostal churches.

In 1654, Reverend John Eliot reported that "three of them [New Englanders] had gotten severall quarts of strong water and with these Liquors, did not onely make themselves drunk, but got a Child of eleven yers of age, the Son of Toteswamp, whom his Father had sent for a little Corne and Fish to that place near Watertowne, where they were. Unto this Child they first gave too [two] spoonfuls of Strong-water, which was more than his head could bear; and another of them put a Bottle, or such like Vessel to his mouth, and cause him to drink till he was very drunk...Now we will see whether your Father [Toteswamp] will punish us for drunkenness for he is a Ruler among them [the Indians]." [183]

The Church Elders judged the three men to "sit in the stocks a good space of time, and thence to be brought to the whipping-Post, and have each of them twenty lashes." [184] And the punishment for the eleven year-old boy: "put in the stocks a little while, and the next day his father was to whip *him in the School, before the Children there* [emphasis added]; all which Judgment was executed." [185]

Church Divines, including Richard Baxter in *Christian Directory* advised children to get on their knees after punishment and entreat "God to bless and sanctify its effect, that it may do you good." [186]

By almost any analysis, the Puritan children were considered to be rebellious, evil, self-loving, stubborn, prideful, and godless. Bruce C. Daniels in *Puritans at Play,* said "the philosophy and reality of child-rearing and the empirical evidence from diaries, autobiographies, and other literary artifacts suggest that much "guilt, anxiety, and low self-esteem" were produced before children reached the age of six." [187] Daniels continues, "the pattern was psychologically devastating and hostile to the development of a personality that could be comfortable experiencing joy and sensuous gratification." [188]

Conquering self-love was a major problem for the Puritan children as they became adolescents and young adults. [Note: adolescence was not known as a period of growth in children during the Puritan period. In fact, it may be only one hundred years old. Puritan childhood stretched from birth to marriage making the "child" subservient to his or her parents past the age of thirty for some.]

Because of the rigid standards established by the Puritan church and practiced in the home, the children were not spontaneous or creative.

At the onset of puberty, the adolescent faced additional guilt and anxiety about their genitals and their interest in self-pleasuring activities. Pleasure, regardless of how it was achieved, was considered to be sinful. Moreover, adolescent males were encouraged to stay in the homes of their parents until age thirty---just as Christ did [or allegedly did].

An additional source of Puritan child guilt was the fact that during adolescence and its typical and predictable behaviors, youths were adopted out to other families to complete the raising of them---not necessarily for any apprenticeship or labor. Morgan, as ill-advised as it is, said "Psychologically...separation [adopted out] of parents and children may have had a *sound foundation*. [emphasis added] The child left home just at the time when parental discipline causes increasing friction, just the time when a child begins to assert his independence." [189] [This information seems to contradict the information that apprenticeships were the reason children were adopted out.]

Separation of parents and children at the critical times during infancy to adulthood, is rarely a "sound foundation." It is difficult to understand how a historian of Morgan's stature could make such a statement about separation being sound.

It was suggested by the Church Divines that separation of children would lessen the chance that they would become too attached to their parents and parents would not cave in to less stringent behavioral requirements. The knowledge of this 'adopt out' practice further would tend to discredit Edmond Morgan's theory of "Puritan Tribalism." Other cultures were more cohesive than the Puritans. There cannot be a tribe if there are no members. But the family was the basis for control of all aspects of spiritual, educational, and spiritual life. In respect to tribalism, Morgan suggests that it was responsible for sustaining the vitality of the church. Conversely, then, it could be said that the lack of tribalism by the migration westward away from family, economic gains, land acquisition, and the desire for a less rigid society, resulted in the rather sudden drop in church membership as well as a decline of the Puritan period generally.

Education was a very important segment of Puritan life. Besides the congregations requiring that clergy be well-educated, the clergy demanded it from the church families for the sake of the children [and the church].

The Massachusetts General Court in 1642 required the town selectmen to assess the parents, masters, and children, whether they could read and understand the laws of the Massachusetts Bay Colony and the doctrines of religions. Reading, writing, and Bible were responsibilities of the parents. As established earlier, a majority of the emigrants could read and write. But when they could not, the parents were required to hire a literate town woman to teach youngsters. Just as in Old England, these schools were called "Dame Schools." By 1647, a law was passed in the Massachusetts Bay Colony called *The Olde Deluder Act of 1647* that required towns of over one hundred homes to establish and pay for the cost of schools. The law to require schools was a "step toward creating a universal education system." [190]

At first only young men, entering at age seven or eight, were provided an education. However, by the end of the Seventeenth Century, girls also were admitted. Some Puritan children were able to read at age three or four with many learning to read Latin by age six. Because of the importance of salvation, learning to read at the earliest possible time would help them learn the Bible. The reading of the Bible was necessary for salvation.

If learning to read was important, so was work---at an even earlier age. It was not uncommon for children to be doing "age appropriate" work [according to the Puritans] in or around the home. In these cases, the work activities were mostly domestic: washing, carrying water, making candles, keeping the fire burning, helping with a younger sibling, and other simple tasks.

The period between puberty and adulthood that we now call "adolescence" as a descriptor did not exist. The Puritan society placed adult thinking and working demands upon children as young as two. They were miniature adults. Without specific court records related to the age of adolescence or diaries specific to the ages twelve to sixteen, one can only suspect that the Puritan teenagers were current teenagers in terms of needs but a long way from the Twenty-first Century in terms of occupational choices, higher education pursuits, social life, and other opportunities. Young Puritan men at age sixteen were eligible for military duty, and if not already apprenticed for learning a trade, were helping with the family farm.

Clearly, adolescence was not the age range for receiving 'freeman' status. As Demos pointed out in *A Little Commonwealth,* "...no set age brought admission to freemanship." [191] The sample [used by Demos] spreads out across a broad range from twenty-five to forty years for the receipt of freeman status.

Nothing additional about courtship and marriage of the children of the Puritan emigrant founders was cited by Demos. That is, it is suspected that there was no dating, no dances, or other forms of social settings whereby a couple might explore compatibility for marriage. Many New England marriages, especially ones of the second generation, occurred within the confines of the first towns with individuals known to each other through church or school. In some cases, the second generation children who were teenagers when they emigrated married other second generation children who they knew in Old England. For certain, the male's family would assist in selecting, discussing and approving a mate for their son. Children needed to marry within their social class. It was customary for Puritan fathers to approve or disapprove of marriage partners at least until the son was twenty or twenty-one years of age.

While the interest in marrying seems to the reader like a business deal, usually a couple had expressed an interest in each other. "The average age of marriage for second generation adults was for males, twenty-five, and for females, twenty-three." [192] Whether there was romantic flirtation or sexual interest depended upon individuals, gender, and social class of the family.

In order to assure parental authority over the marriage of couples, a law was passed that instructed, "If any shall make any motion of marriage to any man's daughter or mayde [maid] servant not having first obtained leave and consent of the parents or master so to doe [he] shalbe punished by a fine or corporall punishment or both." [193]

Marriage was not a religious rite in Puritan New England like it was in Old England. The civil marriage ceremony, sometimes held in the office or home of a Magistrate, also could be held in the home of the bride.

Family in the Puritan period was not unlike the Commonwealth itself: it had God, it had laws, it had government; it had punishment; it had subordinates (children, servants, wives). For sure, the family had order. The husband/father was the patriarch of the family. It was in the family that children were first introduced to the rigors of religion. It was the parents who taught the children to read and write. And, it was the parents who taught the children skills needed for work and survival. But it was the shift in "family government administration" about 1650 from the father to the mother that made all of the difference in moving the family to modernization. While the parental will did not change, the overall effect of mother-led families made it impossible to return to a more rigid, uncaring, solemn, brutish type of child rearing.

This has been said before but is worth repeating: The Puritan adults were scolded in church to treat their children in disciplined ways, but once in the privacy of their homes, such advice was apparently ignored.

The childrearing of the Puritans was transformed over a sixty-year period. By the beginning of the 1670s, the "modern" family in New England was beginning to emerge.......ever so slightly. As the emigrants and the first generation experienced this so-called evolution of love for their children, the issues of infant damnation and children's sinful nature were uppermost in the minds of the adults. Blanket acceptance of theology had given way to enlightenment all because of parental love of their children.

This newfound sensibility about childrearing did not come without challenges from the Calvinist devotees. Expressions of "love" abound in diaries but the evidence of saying how much a Puritan child was loved did not always translate into loving behavior on the part of the father or mother.

In contrast to diaries, wills have been an excellent resource for expressions of love. Humphrey Johnson and Abigail Johnson of Hingham, Massachusetts on July 20, 1688 wrote "We Humphrey Johnson and Abigail my wife in the Township of Hingham in the County of Suffolk, NE is consideration of the <u>love and natural affection which we hear</u>

[have] unto our children John and Deborah Johnson do absolutely confirm to our Son John Johnson and Deborah Johnson all that our hundred acres of land in Scituate called Burnt Plaine as it is confirmed. [Note: Humphrey Johnson, son of Captain John Johnson of Roxbury was ten years of age when he came with his father and siblings to Roxbury on the *Arbella* in 1630. He was married first to Ellen Cheney in 1641 at age twenty-one and to Abigail (Stanfield) May, widow of Samuel May, at age forty-eight. John Johnson was born November 17, 1680 and Deborah Johnson was born June 8, 1682.]

Seventy years later, Reverend Timothy Dwight [1751-1817], a late Calvinist preacher, provided significant theories and new ideas regarding the love of children and child psychology as early as 1773. As Slater said, "Timothy Dwight's child psychology began not with the mind of the child, but with the minds of its progenitors." [194]

Dwight, in his elementary understanding of a child's psyche, never veered from his Orthodox beliefs, but he did manage to cause a shift in the main parenting responsibility from the father to the mother. This shift did not mean that Dwight was soft on discipline. To the contrary, Dwight required "that they [the parents] employ sharp punishments when the occasion warranted." [195]

Even as harsh as it may seem today, Dwight did effect a change in physical punishment based on age appropriateness for the time following below: [196]

- For younger children: the rod

- For older children: reproof, disgrace, confinement, ostracism, and/or denial of privileges.

146

Finally, with Dwight's belief in the value of the child, his theories acted as a transition of total dependency upon the parents to responsible self-direction capable of thinking, judging, comparing, and behaving.

Unfortunately, Timothy Dwight did not begin formulating his child-rearing theories until the late 1770s, leaving thousands of Puritan children in New England between 1630 and 1775 under the stern, rigid and nearly loveless rule of the Orthodox Calvinist leaders and parents.

Dwight's mix of Enlightenment views with his Puritan-Calvinist precepts moved the fledging nation to a better understanding of child-parent relationships, but also moved families toward modernization. Perhaps his greatest gift was helping young people correct the inescapable wrong ideas about God that prevailed until the 1700s---of a harsh and stern judge instead of a loving, benevolent father.

In some households, grandparents and grandchildren were intermixed for reasons of help for the family or help for the grandparents. This cross-generational scene could have had a positive effect upon the care of the children in the household. Grandparents were described as more affectionate and more lenient [in their old age] toward their children's children. [On the other hand, Orthodox Puritans often accused grandparents of corrupting grandchildren by their indulgences.] Of course, we now recognize that cross-generational families still exist, generally with good effect on the children as the grandparents may serve as mediators between the two younger generations, as supportive listeners to the grandchildren, as transmitters of family (and religious) history and traditions to the grandchildren. It is likely that the once harsh and restrictive Puritan grandparents served in a different capacity to their grandchildren.

In some cases, grandchildren helped take care of elderly or infirm grandparents. This was the case in Roxbury, Massachusetts, in the Captain John Johnson household. Cousins Elizabeth Johnson Bowen [daughter of John Johnson's son, Isaac Johnson] and Mehitable Johnson, [daughter of Humphrey Johnson and brother of Isaac Johnson] lived with Captain John Johnson and his third wife, Grace Negus Fawer Johnson. When John Johnson died, they were provided five pounds each in John Johnson's will. [Elizabeth was twenty-two years old and eight months pregnant at the time of Captain John Johnson's death in 1659. [She was married to Henry Bowen in 1658]. Mehitable was fifteen at the time of Captain John Johnson's death, and was married to Samuel Hinsdale at age sixteen.]

The modernization of the New England society slowly moved forward in all aspects: economic, social, education, religion, and governmental. Modernization, as a factor in declination of the Puritan period, is discussed more fully in Chapter Nine.

The Age of Enlightenment of the Eighteenth Century focused centrally upon humanizing religion. All philosophies of this time rejected the notion of original sin and the depravity of infants and children. Simply, the change was from reason based upon faith in the Puritan period to a faith based upon reason by the mid-1700s. Enlightenment had more to do with changing New England and the Puritans than did the Reformation and Calvin. It is believed that Puritan parents in the late Seventeenth Century privately held the view that their children were not depraved and were not destined for Hell as the Church Divines told them. Reason provided relief from the stress of damnation of the children and changed religious thought and practice forever.

Perhaps in the final analysis, it will be found that it was the Puritan children [after all] who by rejecting the Mathers' and Cotton's *New England Way,* confirmed the failure of the Puritan experiment by not returning to the ways that Cotton and other [and later] Church Divines hoped could have been.

Kaufmann, in *Institutional Individualism,* firmly establishes that Puritan individuals not only exerted influence by making the choices about the institutions they would join, but also re-examined their relationships to patriarchal authority in the family, church, and civil hierarchy.

Finally, Kaufmann, may be telling us caretakers of history, that each generation and each self needs to be cautious in perceiving history. Hoping for what could have been or a return to what was becomes a longing for, as Kaufmann states, "Something we never fully possess: the self we never were, the self we will never be." [197]

CHAPTER THIRTEEN

PSYCHOLOGICAL AND SOCIAL PROBLEMS OF GROWING UP PURITAN

Child-rearing practices by the Emigrant founders in the Massachusetts Bay Colony were, for the most part, rigid, repressive, and restrictive. These harsh practices were very characteristic in the Fourteenth to Eighteenth Centuries. One way that the psychological and social impact of the Puritan founders' child-rearing practices had an effect on the children was how the children were prepared for adulthood and parenting.

Psychological and social damage in Colonial America is difficult to determine, however, since the language of present-day psychologists and social workers did not exist in the Seventeenth Century.

Certain "sins," for example, may in fact have been mental health problems but they were classified as sins and were punished as such. Social class differences and gender also determined one's sins and their punishments during this time period. Diaries of adults are less reliable than those of the children. And, biographies and autobiographies do not always reflect the truth. Reverend Cotton Mather, as an illustration, wrote a biography about his grandfather, Reverend Richard Mather. The biography was full of perceptions of good and positive things Richard Mather did in his lifetime. And, the biography reflected an estimation of what Cotton Mather's father [Increase Mather] thought of his father, Richard Mather. *Cotton Mather was only six years old when his grandfather, Richard Mather, died.*

As Robert Middlekauff said in *The Mathers*, "Richard stands as the noble exile, banished to the wilderness of America for his devotion to the true church order." [198]

Likewise, Cotton Mather wrote a glowing account of his maternal grandfather, Reverend John Cotton, yet John Cotton did more to damage the children by his rigid, repressive, and unbending nature. Cotton Mather did not have the understanding to be able to sort out what was good, fair, and right even though he observed what was happening in the Puritan society [that he attributed to the lack of conversion and piety.]

Exempt from this discussion are mental health issues that are medically and physiologically founded such as mental retardation, cerebral palsy, epilepsy, and similar disabilities. Also excluded from this section are those extreme religious groups such as the Quakers, whose "dancing and shaking" and other behaviors were thought by the Puritans to be "crazy." The Quakers violated several Puritan customs but these violations would not be considered mental problems today.

Identified by Bruce C. Daniels in *The Puritans at Play,* are the following descriptors or characteristics that support the perception of what Puritan children and youth experienced in the Seventeenth Century:

> Shame, guilt, anxiety, low self-esteem, over manipulation, hostility, over developed superegos, compromised egos, suicide, despair, terror, crazy, crazy-brained, idiot, deluded, lunatic, mad, distracted, distempered, fits [may have been medical] possessed, insane, obsessive, compulsive, rage, infantile anxiety, separation, and, trauma.

Lacking in the Colonial records is what the Puritans used for evidence to declare a person "mad," or as we might conclude today, "emotionally disturbed," or "mentally ill." Further, there are few records of treatment. "Thomas Smith was put in jail for two years by the Suffolk County Magistrates for *drunkenness and madness* after he put his wife and children in fear of their lives in 1679." [199] In today's society, he might be charged with abuse, neglect, or even menacing but would have been referred to an alcohol treatment program at the least.

"Idiots" as the Puritans called people who were merely "simple," caused enough concern in the Colony because laws were passed to deal with this type of "mental illness." "Indecisiveness" was sometimes classified or suggested as a mental problem. But for the most part, the Puritans would classify any behavior that seemed bizarre or erratic as a mental problem or a mind problem. Many times those who were close to death exhibited behaviors as they went in and out of conscience that would prompt statements in diaries and records about "terror," "mad," or "lunatic."

In nearly all references to "fits" there was usually some reference to falling down or falling sickness. Of course, today this epileptic seizure is considered a medical problem not a mental one.

Women did not escape classification of behaviors that could be called mental illness. In fact, women over all were more frequently cited in the Puritan records than men. And, adults made up most of those who were labeled in such a way that one could conclude they were mentally ill by today's standards. Children, except for "idiots," escaped being labeled.

By 1660, the Magistrates generally used some of the terms referenced on the second page of this chapter instead of concluding that a Colonist had committed a crime. Sometimes Puritans and non-Puritans escaped the usual references but might be called a "witch" or "bewitched."

Governor John Winthrop made reference to a family who left the Massachusetts Bay Colony noting that "one daughter was mad and two other daughters had been sexually abused by "lewd persons" and "filthiness" in his family." [200] Winthrop did not understand the psychological consequences of sexual abuse. Instead, he merely stated that in this case "one daughter was mad."

As Larry D. Eldridge commented in his article, "Crazy-Brained: Mental Illness in Colonial America," "Whatever the causes of mental illness as colonists understood them, or as present-day observers might interpret them, the consequences [for Colony, Town, and family] could be significant." [201]

Caring for mentally ill people in the homes of relatives proved to be a financial and emotional burden. Besides, the physical danger to the family was a significant factor. The mentally ill person usually lingered in a prolonged state of existence without appropriate care [if there had been any].

From the Wish edition of *The Diary of Samuel Sewell,* on August 12, 1676, "just as prayer ended Timothy Dwight sank down in a Swoun, and for a good space was as if he perceived not what done to him: after, kicked and sprawled, knocking his hands and feet upon the floor like a distracted man." [202] [Apparently, Timothy Dwight's distraction arose from fear of sin regarding a maid whom he passionately loved. In the Seventeenth Century distraction was used to describe a multitude of mental and emotional problems.]

Samuel Sewell, himself, had considerable self-doubt. In 1678, he reports in his diary that he assumed that he was unfit for entering the Roxbury Church because Reverend Walter said "nothing of my coming into the church nor wished God to show me grace therein...but I never experienced more unbelief." [203]

Margaret Cheany [Cheney] wife of William Cheney thanked God on March 24, 1673, confessing and bewailing her sinful yielding to temptation for "loosing her chain of the melancholick distemper [which she had for ten or eleven years following the death of her husband, William Cheney] which made her wholly neglect her Calling & live mopishly." [204] Margaret's son, Thomas Cheney, left his Cambridge, Massachusetts farm for several years to take care of his mother prior to her recovery from her mental illness.

The New England towns from the beginning were responsible for inhabitants within the boundaries of the towns. Those who were strangers in the towns were provided "warning out" notices to leave the towns. In this way, towns limited their expenditures to only the "accepted" residents of the towns. Mentally ill people were not warned out by the town authorities but were maintained by them. *The Massachusetts Body of Liberties of 1641* required towns to care for its citizens at community expense. In 1678, the Massachusetts Bay Colony Magistrates reaffirmed this.

Because the Puritans did not believe that "madness" could be cured or corrected by medical treatment, little else was done to help those who were mentally ill except for prayer, fasting, and in some cases, blood letting. There were isolated cases of bizarre treatment in the Seventeenth Century but records of their success are not documented.

Eldridge found "no significant differences in the kinds or numbers of mentally ill in the Seventeenth Century Colonies over time, and he saw no long-term changes in the way that such people were viewed or treated." [205]

However, Eldridge did find that the relationship "between mental illness and religion was stronger in the Puritan stronghold in the Massachusetts Bay Colony than in the Middle or Southern Colonies." [206]

Records of the Massachusetts Bay Colony are somewhat misleading regarding social status and/or wealth. For example, poorer people were more frequently documented in court actions than wealthier people. It is believed that this happened because the poorer people needed town or Colony resources for their mentally ill family member more than the wealthier family.

Over all, the Puritans provided respectable care and treatment for the mentally ill in their towns for the time period. The Puritans' concept of God's Grace probably strengthened their sense of responsibility and their concern for their mentally ill family member.

While the Puritans otherwise have been exposed by early America historians for their stern, rigid persona, they were compassionate and caring toward the mentally ill. Clearly, they did the best they could with the limited understanding of the causes and treatment of the types of symptoms we now call mental illness.

In Samuel Sewell's *Diary*, he indicated various mental illnesses in Boston:

> "April 4, 1688 -At night Sam. Marion's wife
> hangs herself in the Chamber, fastening a Cord

to the Rafter-Joice. Two or three swore she was *distracted*, and had been for some time...." [207]

"January 26, 1686, Sewall wrote that Cousin Fissenden tells me there is a Maid in Woburn who 'tis feared in *Possessed* by an evil Spirit." [208]

And, January 19, 1694, "Mrs. Prout dies after *conflicts of the mind*, not without suspicion of Witchcraft." [209]

Poor Sarah Stevens was committed to prison in 1687 for "lying with Christopher Lawson." But upon further examination by the Suffolk County Court, she was, "by judging her carriages and testimonies concerning her, "discharged because she was a "distempered, crazy woman." [210]

In the early Nineteenth Century, Dr. Benjamin Rush, a medical doctor who was interested in issues of mental illness wrote:

> "...*madness* is excited in the understanding most frequently by impressions that act primarily upon the heart...joy, love, fear, grief, distress, shame from offended delicacy, defamation and calumny."

Rush continues that,

> "grief and guilt resulting from infidelity or sexual incontinence were other potential causes of madness."

157

In the family history of *Mary Moody Emerson and Transcendentalism* by Phyllis Cole, it is cited that Reverend Joseph Emerson appeared before his congregation in Malden "wearing a white handkerchief over his face, falling rapidly thereafter into severe and disabling sorrow." [211] The only reference to his illness in surviving family papers hints at the degree of concern by Joseph Emerson, Junior who noted in his diary "that his parents had visited York expressly to see their beloved friend and brother but found him very *Malancholy*." It is thought that Reverend Joseph Emerson was experiencing "religious depression."

But, what about mental illness of the Puritan children? Did it exist? Except for very brief comments in the records of the Massachusetts Bay Colony, children [estimated to be under twenty years of age] exhibited similar types of symptoms of mental illness as the Puritan adults but the 'cause' was most generally attributed to sinful activities.

Puritans sought, "with varying degrees of success, to remold themselves into what we would now call an obsessive-compulsive" personality, and their religion into obsessive ordering," according to David Leverenz. [212]

Leverenz continues to describe the Puritans as "the most aggressive, self-confident, and self-demanding of all this mechanical class---as well as the most self-doubting and insecure..." [213]

In the world of Puritanism, even though the home was paternally governed, the real father was God, the stern father. Many a Puritan father was self-punishing and had strong feelings of guilt in regard to being a weak father and not being a good example for his sons. It is suspected that the feeling of failure as a father was a lack of understanding of the adolescent. Rarely was doubt recorded about infants or small children...just rebellious adolescents. The Puritan father did not understand that children and adolescents were not miniature adults let alone miniatures of their fathers or even their mothers. How father failure affected the children is yet to be uncovered.

Children [Leverenz believes this means pre-teens] were disciplined according to virtually every book written in the early Seventeenth Century about "duties of the parents." Techniques such as isolation, beatings, and whippings used to break the will of the child [as recommended by early Church Divines] would be considered child abuse today.

Cole, in her book on *Mary Moody Emerson and Transcendentalism* provides an excellent example from the diary of Joseph Moody, son of Samuel and Hannah Moody that establishes the paternal wrath and provocation of fear. He stated, "At noon my father grew very angry...revealing a volatile emotional life." [214] Joseph continues about himself by saying, "he had internalized his father's pleas for conversion from the slavery of sin but instead of progressing toward his work, he recorded forbidden behaviors and feelings and admitted to hostility toward God and toward his work as well as lustful feelings toward a variety of women and many times 'self-defiling.'" [215] Leverenz suggests, "The Puritan family was sending a pervasive mixed signal to its young: feel nourished and valued, yet feel sinful and ashamed." [216]

The mixed signals representing contradictory poles [the confusion of the double bind] as stated in the previous paragraph has been suggested as possible reasons for schizophrenia and sure, pervasive ambivalence. With self-worth and self-trust compromised by the rigid and repressive father [in spite of a more nurturing mother], the male children developed feelings of shame, sin, and guilt. Female children, luckily, could follow in the steps of their mothers without much interference from their fathers.

Because of the Biblical and cultural heritage of the Puritans, male children had to change so they represented what the father in the family expected. Disciplined male children then would be able to revere the Heavenly Father in the manner required by the Puritans based upon what they believed the Bible said about their male roles and about what the Old Testament provides for males versus females.

John Dod and Robert Cleaver joined forces in 1603 and published a book called *A Godlye Form of Household Government.* This Puritan "family advice book" provided in straightforward fashion how parents should provide childcare, and in particular, what roles the mother and the father should be. The book in characteristically Puritan form, advises Puritans that "Parents who disobey the duties described in *Godlye Form of Household Government,* will find that God's wrath is shown in punishing disobedience with disobedience. [217] In other words, if parents neglected their duties by not disciplining their children, the children would be rebellious and disobedient.

Parents were terrorized they would not provide stern enough discipline because rebellion from the children meant sinfulness in the parents.

From the Cole book we learn about stern discipline from Mary Moody as she states, "I remember my Father's punishing me once. I was two years old and when I came into his study I wouldn't make my curtsy...so he whipped me. Mother came in and asked why he had punished me. He said "Because she wouldn't make her duty on coming into the room." "What! Whip a child two years old for that!"

My Father said, 'My dear, since you have interfered I must whip her again, and he did." [218] As Cole points out, "Women were not classed with children and servants in the language of covenant, but neither were they equal partners in the affirming or enforcing of family government." [219]

At the same time, Dod and Cleaver were advocating a more reasonable balance between harsh discipline by the father and loving nurture by the mother. The confusion must have been horrendous for the children.

Leverenz sums it up best when he said, "The precepts and practical examples of duties make it clear that good mothers were tender, so were the young children; good fathers were grave, so were good *older* children." [220]

Reverend Cotton Mather [1663-1728] wrote *Duties of Parents to Children.* The same stern advice was given to the New England Puritans about childrearing as was given eighty years earlier by Dod and Cleaver.

The pressure by the Church Divines on the Puritan parents was tremendous. It was absolutely necessary that the children be godly and the way to godliness was by way of harsh discipline. It is interesting to note that the advice by Dod and Cleaver about the rebellious children [teens] was to give them less love, not more. The withdrawal of affection and love occurred about at the same time the Puritan father's harsh disciplinary role was assumed.

Harvey Wish, an Elbert Jay Benton Distinguished Professor of American History at Western Reserve University and editor of the *Diary of Samuel Sewell* (Putnams Sons), states that Sewall was "obsessed with death and funerals, and made his children neurotic on the subject." [221] [One son was Sam Sewell, an alcoholic who had substantial marriage problems]

Post-Freudian studies of Harry S. Sullivan and Melanie Klein noted that "Puritan children's obsessive feelings begin not simply with the father's discipline, but with early responses to a mother who at once was loving, demanding, and then rejecting." [222]

Regardless of whether Puritan children experienced too much or too little mother love or too much or too little father discipline, the variety of rebellious activities and the types of mental health issues cited at the beginning of this chapter are overwhelming.

The movement to modernization meant rejection of the adherence to God the Father, and father the person, resulted in individualism, trust in self, and expressiveness. The second generation could not escape the feelings of patriarchal control and possessiveness.

The Epilogue by psychologist Dr. Lita Linzer Schwartz discusses further why the Puritan adults felt so desperate and how the family and community dynamics of the time affected the children.

CHAPTER FOURTEEN

A SUMMARY OF FINDINGS

Any effort to summarize findings in order to reach possible conclusions will surely require specificity as well as some generalization.

This summary includes pertinent information about children, adolescents, adults, church, religious history of beliefs and practices, Theocratic government, laws, parenting, the Church Divines in New and Old England, population, and mental health problems that either individually or collectively affected the outcome of the culture and society called Puritan. The main assumption is that the effect of the total environment in the Puritan period affected the children and grandchildren of the Emigrant founders to the extent that decisions about church, self, and society were easily made and adapted to by the children and grandchildren.

The First Church of Roxbury, 1631-1670 had only four ministers. These were Thomas Weld(e), John Eliot, Nehemiah Walther, and Samuel Danforth. Examination of sermons and books of these four ministers did not reveal any theological changes throughout the forty-year study period. In fact, the issues of infant baptism, child damnation, church membership, halfway covenant, and the place of children in general did not change for forty years. Children, in particular, did not have the experience of communion, or conversion, and did not on the whole, choose to join the Roxbury church.

The concept of Original Sin was an important cornerstone of the church. The guilt of "passing on the original sin of Adam" by way of sexual intercourse had a dramatic effect upon the Puritan attitude about sexual matters. More importantly, the children who resulted from the sexual union of Puritan parents were "born with original sin."

The numerous examples of written evidence in sermons, books, and diaries, provide dependable and reliable evidence that the Puritan religion was a rigid and repressive religion based mostly upon the Old Testament. Once the Puritans were isolated in New England, the religion and the society became even more fundamental, more rigid, and more negative.

The *Massachusetts Body of Liberties of 1641* set forth adaptations of English law, and included many new laws developed by and for the Puritans themselves. Puritans always saw the civil government as an agent of support for the Church. Therefore, it is not surprising to find that the laws, especially for capital offenses, are reflective of Bible scripture to justify the law and the punishment of the offence.

The laws in the Massachusetts Bay Colony were applied equally to Puritans and non-Puritans but the application of punishment depended upon social class and position within the Puritan community. More court records, for example, exist for people in the middle and lower social classes than for the Gentry class. [The pattern of penalties for privileged persons in current societies is not much different from what the Puritans experienced in the Seventeenth Century.] While the Magistrates used some discretion, children who committed offenses were tried nonetheless alongside adults.

Dr. Roger Thompson, East Anglia University Professor, in *Sex in Middlesex*, suggests a different slant on the rejection of the church by the children and grandchildren of the Emigrant Founders. He reports that "Philip Greven (*The*

Protestant Temperment, New York, 1977), in reviewing Puritan spiritual autobiographies, described how over and over again the recollections of evangelicals reveal the emergence during youth and early adulthood of a growing sense of selfhood and self will, an increasing confidence that they can act on their own behalf and for their own purposes apart from the expectations set for them by parents or others.[223]

While parenting/child-rearing skills varied from family to family, the Puritan Church Divines had an overwhelming influence on establishing the "duties of parents to children" resulting in the stern, rigid, and repressive discipline from the father. Mothers provided nurture and love at least up to the age of twelve.

Primarily, the goal of parenting [at least for the male children] was to bring them to godliness, conversion, confession, and church membership. To do less meant that the father was a failure. The children were often exposed to contradictory poles of affection: nourished on the one hand; beaten on the other hand.

The Puritan father and mother did not understand the psychological make-up of pubescent and adolescent youth. The sense of individualism, inquiry, interest in sexual matters, and rebellion made some parents adopt out their unruly, rebellious youth to another family to rear.

Children, over all, were considered to be depraved vipers from the moment of birth. It is believed that not all parents felt this way. In fact, the suggestion has been made that it was likely parents heard one thing in church but practiced differently once in the home. This, apparently, was especially true regarding the issue of infant damnation.

Children by the age of two were required to work at tasks in the home. They were instructed as early as possible from the Bible and various catechisms, and were taught to read at an early age so they could read the Bible.

Because the Puritan society in New England was physically isolated from the rest of the world, it became known as a "closed society." However, in reality, there were frequent contacts with travelers from England and with New England travelers who went to England. Additionally, there were contacts with those on trading ships from Spain, Portugal and other countries that stopped in the Massachusetts Bay. But the physical distance, especially from England, made it possible for the development of the "New Israel" that the Puritans believed to be their destiny.

The relative isolation did not permit the Puritans to connect to the rest of the world and that isolation delayed modernization of the society, family, and self. Restrictive religions, like the Puritans had, did not allow knowledge of other religions [except the Roman Catholic religion about which they had considerable disdain], humanities, or even modern critical thought. Furthermore, it is believed that the Puritan Commonwealth increased the social and cultural isolation because of the many prohibitions that it had about theater, dance, dress, and music.

It is believed by current psychologists that when the tenets of a restrictive, repressive religious group [like the Puritans] serve as the primary and only source of self-definition and meaning, the result for church members, non-church members yet to join, and children can be mental depression. This author believes this is especially true of the non-converted children and grandchildren who did not join the church but were well aware that their Emigrant founder parents and grandparents had identity, purpose, and meaning as Elect or Visible Saints. The influx of non-Puritan emigrants, some who were fortune seekers, brought additional problems to the Colony such as poverty, crime, and education. But non-Puritans also brought skilled labor and wealth to the Massachusetts Bay Colony. By 1645, the Puritans were outnumbered four to one by the non-Puritans. This in itself perplexed the Puritans regarding land grants, freeman status, voting, serving in civil positions and business ownership and profit making.

Threatening the children with hell and withholding salvation for all but the Elect, likely caused anxiety, guilt, and conflicting loyalty to a growing sense of self. It has been suggested that this fear of damnation, the lack of suitability for conversion, and the constant watchfulness by the Puritan neighbors, led to mental exhaustion as well as physical problems.

From time to time, "Puritan" is shown in groupings of cults or sects. However, while the beliefs and practices of the Puritans were "doomsday," controlling, restrictive, repressive, rigid, and by today's standard, non-democratic, the term Puritan does not fit the present-day accepted theological definitions of cult. [see *www.religioustolerance.org/cults.htm* for definitions.]

Nonetheless, the way of life, religiously and personally, for the Puritans in New England likely was depressing, if not very difficult, for most of the children and grandchildren of the Emigrant Founders. Most all aspects of their lives were affected by the Puritan beliefs and practices: behavior, thought, emotion, sex, environment, religious status, personal status, work, land ownership, separation from parents, conformity, dependency, and even abuse.

According to Reverend Ken Steigler, a [current] Methodist pastor in Salem, Massachusetts, the "comfort of having someone tell you what is right and what is wrong, in time, becomes a psychological prison." [224]   Lonnie D. Kliever, a cult expert and chairman of the religion department at Southern Methodist University in Dallas, Texas says "...controlling churches can be attractive ...because people [nowadays] join such congregations as they search for self-identity." [225]   It is unlikely in the early- to mid-1600s that Puritan children were searching for self-identity inasmuch as their identity was pretty well determined for them. But by the 1670s, the children and grandchildren of the Puritan emigrants were beginning to explore their individualism and freedoms in the time and context of the declining Puritan society.

The dark side of Puritan history was [and continues to be in present-day fundamentalist organizations] control of one's personal freedom and one's faith practices and beliefs. The effort by the Puritan Church Divines to require obedience to their interpretation of the word of God and to conformity within the Puritan community and government [including family government] led to a system of punishment for most who disobeyed.   The punishment varied, however, depending upon class, gender, and crime.

The differentiation made by the Seventeenth Century civil and church government in the Massachusetts Bay Colony between males and females, children and adults, native Americans and whites, Negro slaves and masters, Calvinism and other beliefs, educated and non-educated, upper class and lower class, merchants and farmers resulted in compromised individual freedoms to say the least. It is well documented that neither the early government nor the early Seventeenth Century Puritan Church Divines ever believed in the value of personal freedom. What is not well documented in records of the Colony is whether the children and grandchildren of the Emigrant Founders were actively seeking individual freedom or democracy as we now know it. We do understand, however, that successive generations appear to have discarded many points of view of their ancestors about religion and their society that were no longer believed or accepted, and did modify other aspects from the heritage of their Emigrant relatives. This modification or rejection resulted in more personal autonomy and freedom for the younger generations.

The Seventeenth Century Puritan children and grandchildren were not unlike those of the same age in other countries and cultures. It seems all generations of children become exiled from *part* of their past beliefs and practices, and from their parents, as they move toward modernization of their own life and family.

In regard to the religious practices and beliefs of current fundamental churches, it must be remembered that they have many of the characteristics of the Puritans. As allegedly deceptive and psychologically dangerous as these fundamental churches seem to be, people join religious organizations for different reasons than did the Puritans. Clearly, from the enormous evidence of early American history, the Puritans joined the Puritan churches for different reasons than the reasons people today who join fundamental groups.

However, selected from a variety of sources (Fischer, Morgan, Miller, Greven), the following descriptive words reflect possible damage in today's context to the emotional and psychological health of the Puritan children:

Guilt	Anxiety	low self-esteem
over manipulation	Hostility	over developed superegos
compromised egos	Suicide	despair
Terror	Crazy	crazy-brained
Idiot	Deluded	lunatic
Mad	distracted	distempered
Fits	possessed	insane
Obsessive	compulsive	Rage
infantile anxiety	separation	trauma

The following Puritan Child Profile, with some exceptions, is offered to establish the typical experiences of Puritan children during the period 1630-1670 in the Massachusetts Bay Colony:

Control:

- parents (behavior, religion, work, marriage)

- religion (church attendance, membership, communion)

- community (laws)

Abuse:

- parents (whipping, isolation)

- community (public whipping, ridicule)

- parents (shaming, emotional)

- church (public confession of personal sins)

Feelings:

- terror (death of self and family)

- dismal (soul, redemption)

- scared (Hell, damnation)

- guilt (sex)

- no joyfulness/fun (home, school, community)

- distrust (Puritan hierarchy and world)

- conformity (required by all)

Other Exposures:

- church (4 times a week service; 3 hours on Sunday at least)

- suicides (of other children and adults)

- depression (of self, others)

- sins (of self, others)

- hypocrisy (within church and community

- low self-esteem (self and others)

Other Impacts:

- Puritans were minority in the Colony

- not all children were recognized or valued

- some children were not able to have self-expression

- children had no spontaneity

- no choices available or permitted

- work assigned at an early age

- handed off as teenager for others to complete raising

To some, the restrictive, repressive, and punitive behaviors of the Puritans might seem similar to those of modern-day cults. However, a key difference is that Puritans were not in adulation of and totally submissive to a charismatic leader. Their worship was directed to God. Second, the Puritan preachers did not use unethical manipulative techniques to control their flocks in a totalistic society. Third, similar behaviors were characteristic of other segments of the Protestant Church of the period, such as the Dutch Reformed Church in New Amsterdam under Peter Stuyvesant, and are to be found, even today, in some Protestant denominations. Fourth, what we consider child abuse today was not regarded as such in the Seventeenth Century, or even fifty years ago in our own times. [For a deeper discussion of this particular issue, see Langone and Eisenberg's chapter on "Children and cults" (1993).]

So can Puritan outcomes be predicted based upon a profile or study of the family, parenting, church, community, and civil government? Can Puritan outcomes translate into psychological labels used today? Can comparisons be made between the children of the Puritan period and those children of today? Are there any strong messages about parenting then and today? What are the comparisons of self-confidence and self-esteem today versus those of the Puritan children? What were the long-term mental health issues growing up Puritan? What can be said about the changes in the Church since Enlightenment and the effect upon society?

These are just a few of the questions that Dr. Lita Linzer Schwartz, psychologist, will answer in the Epilogue.

EPILOGUE

As one reads the sermons, laws, history, and descriptions of the Puritans in the preceding pages, it must be remembered that these were some of the few literate "middle-class" peoples in the world four centuries ago. Their literacy was due in part to the printing of the English translations of the Bible, especially the Geneva Bible in the sixteenth century and later the King James version early in the seventeenth century (Bobrick, 2001), which people were about to read for themselves so that they would know the word of God. It must also be remembered that they were risk-takers. Who else would sail across thousands of miles of ocean, for several weeks, to an unknown place filled with who knew what dangers? The desire to leave England was based partly on persecution for their religious views and partly on the desire to leave the turmoil that characterized England in the sixteenth century. Some moved to The Netherlands initially, and then moved on to America where there might be literally and figuratively more space; others came more directly.

The prescriptions and proscriptions proclaimed in the sermons and laws of the Massachusetts Bay Colony were in the service of God as well as that of man, the latter in the sense that order and communal effort were vital to the survival of the Colony in the New World. Breen and Foster (1973) found that the Massachusetts Bay Puritans were able to organize their society based upon a contractual model, the essential ingredient of which was free will. The "individual voluntarily promised to obey civil and scriptural law, for the seventeenth century Puritans believed that meaningful obedience could only grow out of voluntary consent, never out of coercion" (p.12). Further, they decided that the towns and churches would be homogeneous in the sense that dissidents and strangers would be excluded. This theocratic position contributed to social cohesion, peace, and order. The subjection of wives to their husbands' authority had Biblical sanction as well as historical tradition to support it, and parental authority similarly has these twin sources. Neither made much allowance for individual differences as we think of them today, i.e., weak vs. strong male or female figures. Similarly, the injunctions of teaching children the road to follow made little allowance for differences in *their* personalities, or even their pace of development.

As we seek to understand the changes from the first generation of Puritans on these shores to the later ones, we have to remember that 1) we are dealing with data remote in time, some of it possibly modified in content to reflect certain viewpoints, and incomplete in most cases; 2) that not every adult or child followed the prescribed pattern to the last detail; and 3) that those who have studied the Puritan period do not necessarily agree in their views of what occurred at that time. An additional fact to be kept in mind is that historians and other scholars have written about several different communities, not the same one, and that each community differed slightly from the others –had its own *zeitgeist*, as it were.

Individuals differed even then from their siblings and their neighbors, so some might have been more non-conformist than others because of their unique personality development even in the face of the same demands that their siblings met. That alone makes each generation potentially somewhat different from the one that preceded it. Add to that the interaction of a number of factors: the greater geographic mobility available in the Massachusetts Bay Colony as compared to England, the growth of commerce and towns, the accessibility of the frontier, the availability of more land, the interaction with the Native Americans (who, after all, provided a different life-style and different ideas), and, as the years passed, even occasional travelers and marriage with persons from other colonies, and the potential for generational differences is increased simply as a factor of time passing, changing experiences, and the interaction of multiple factors within the environment.

As a psychologist rather than an historian, I am very aware that people report the same event from different perspectives, and that therefore their perceptions are not necessarily uniform. Reading the preceding pages and then interpretations by recognized scholars, these differences become ever more apparent. Even those who are seen as psychohistorians differ in their views, depending on whether their principal influence was the Freudian psychoanalytic school (less common today than was true two to four decades ago), or another one, and whether they were doing their research a few decades ago or more recently.

My training as a psychologist leaned heavily on the work of Kurt Lewin (1951), and I think that his basic formula, developed from the field theory of the physical sciences, had great applicability here:

$$\text{Behavior} = f(P \times E)$$

That is: Behavior is a function of the interaction of the person and the environment. Further, Lewin termed the "field" within which the individual behaves a "life space," which is "the total psychological environment which the person experiences subjectively" (Marrow, 1977, p. 35).

The individual's "psychological environment" is further defined as including memories, beliefs, and unconscious influences as well as needs, goals, and other factors which affect the individual in the present. The Life Space is, in turn, affected by factors or forces, that arise in the larger environment, as seen in Figure 1: "Life-space of the child" on the next page.

Certainly heredity contributes much to the person: physical build and health; the potential for behaviors in many facets of life including intelligence, reaction time, talents for music or art; and so on. However, most of these are also shaped by the external environment: parental nurturing, diet, climate, disease, peace or war, and education, among other elements. One's personality, often demonstrated in behavior, develops from the interaction of these two key factors. From one generation to the next, both factors are modified: heredity because of the blending of genes from two different family strains, and environment because of the changes surrounding and involving the family and the community. That said, each generation evolves from the previous one and is modified by contemporary events and needs to some degree.

I certainly recall being taught in American history courses that the Puritans were rigid, devoid of pleasures, harsh disciplinarians, and had other such negative characteristics. That picture has been altered somewhat by reading the work of many historians and others, as well as the documents included in this volume. Accordingly, I propose to pose some relevant questions about the Puritan society and children and to attempt to answer them based on both the foregoing analyses and contemporary psychological thought.

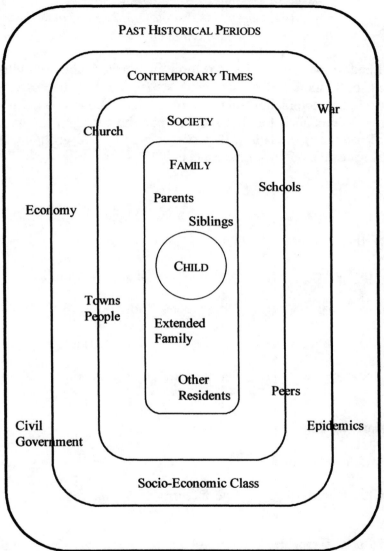

Figure 1
LIFE SPACE OF THE CHILD

PAST HISTORICAL PERIODS

CONTEMPORARY TIMES

SOCIETY

War

Church

FAMILY

Parents

Schools

Siblings

Economy

CHILD

Towns
People

Extended
Family

Other
Residents

Peers

Civil
Government

Epidemics

Socio-Economic Class

The worlds within which the child learns and functions
and which affect the child's life (after Lewin).

- *Can comparisons be made between the children of the Puritan period and the children of today?*

- *Can we compare the social and emotional behavior of Puritan children and today's?*

Although we might try to force-fit Puritan children into Erikson's model, his ages and stages do not necessarily match the actual development of Puritan children but they provide guidance for discussion. For those unfamiliar with Erikson's stages (1963), they are divided by age groups and have positive and negative aspects:

Erikson's Model

Age	Stage
Birth-1 ½ years	Trust vs. mistrust
2 to 4 years	Autonomy vs. shame and doubt
4 to 7 years	Initiative vs. Guilt
7 to 11 or 12 years	Industry vs. Inferiority (latency)
Adolescence	Sense of identity vs. identity diffusion
Early adulthood	Intimacy vs. Isolation
Middle adulthood	Generativity vs. Stagnation
Older adulthood	Ego integrity vs. Despair

Mothers were clearly encouraged to breast-feed in Puritan times, establishing a sense of "being there," necessary for a sense of trust. The breast-feeding might last only a relatively short period, however, if she was pressed to become pregnant frequently. Judith Coffin, wife of Tristam, for example, had ten children in a sixteen-year period (Ulrich, 1991), so had to create the sense of trust in other ways, for "Mothers represented the affectionate mode in an essentially authoritarian system of child-rearing" (p. 154). That nurturing role continued until the child was about ten years old (Leverenz, 1980). Judith Tilden Pabodie had a child every two years over a 15-year period (Courtwright, 1985). This certainly created the setting for sibling rivalry, feelings of jealousy or rejection, and the need for older children to assume more responsibility as additional babies arrived.

There was love of children by parents (Slater, 1977), although it might not have been demonstrated physically for fear of giving the child some kind of false impression of being "better" than others. Indeed, the parents could have seen their children as born in original sin or predestined for damnation and have vented their displeasure at the child's misbehavior by referring to this inborn depravity, but at the same time could love their apparent innocence. Parental affection and authority were better blended in shaping the child's obedience and consciousness (and desire to please a parent) early on than in trying to "break" his spirit a few years later by whippings, but which model was followed varied by family.

In Puritan times, and even among some fundamentalist groups today, the autonomy to be developed in the second stage is outweighed by "shame and doubt," especially "shame" if the child is not obedient. The curiosity and initiative that are normal in Erikson's third stage were and are repressed by heavy doses of guilt for asking questions or exploring behaviors or ideas deemed inappropriate by parents (usually the father), teachers, or others in the community. "Industry" was certainly encouraged in the Puritan family, beginning somewhat earlier in terms of assuming household tasks at a pre-latency age, but that can still be true today in many families, especially farming families. Being apprenticed to another family, allegedly to reduce emotional entanglement with the family or origin as was often done in Puritan times and even into the nineteenth century, is not practiced today; rather it is the adolescent who reaches out to friends as he/she seeks to separate somewhat from the family and to develop a sense of identity. There was, however, a practical purpose to the placement in Puritan times (and later): the youth learned a trade. He gained a potential identity for the future.

The Puritans considered that childhood ended at about age 14, and "youth" extended into the late 20s, although Cotton Mather called himself a youth at age thirty-one (Beales, 1975). Legal responsibility for rebellion, militia service, or marriage was often assumed at age sixteen (Beales, 1975), but marriage rarely took place that early. It should be noted that early adulthood today is seen as ages 20-40 years, depending on whether one is still in school or totally dependent on or independent of parents at the younger end (Colarusso & Nemiroff, 1981). Children are expected to separate psychologically from their parents at the younger end and then to establish an adult relationship with them as they mature. Acquiring marketable skills and choosing a career come in this period, perhaps 5 to 10 years later than the Puritans. Adopting ethical and spiritual roles also comes in this period, perhaps changing over time as the young adult marries or becomes a parent.

Gaining a "sense of identity" would include religious belief and commitment. Although taken regularly to church several times a week and saying prayers several times daily at home, the Puritan child or youth was sometimes not admitted to "membership" in the church until what we would consider young adulthood. Youthful diversion from the "straight and narrow" and lack of admission to the religious communion among the Puritans (Beales, 1975) resembles practices still current among the Old Order Amish, however, who are allowed (subtly encouraged?) as older teenagers to visit a nearby town where they can see films and television, use electricity, ride in a car, and indulge in a number of non-traditional pleasures before being baptized and accepted into the community as adults who uphold and follow Amish doctrine to the letter. As a matter of practice, this "safety-valve" theory seems effective, i.e., "by giving their young people a certain amount of leeway prior to baptism, it is felt that those who do join the church will prove to be loyal and conscientious members: (Kephart & Zellner, 1991, p. 42).

Depending on which source is read, you can find that children were not seen as a separate or special group after the first year or so and that they were regarded as miniature adults, or that they were seen as different. It is clear from reading Harevan (1991), Saveth (1969), and others that there is no unanimity among students of American family history as to the role of children in seventeenth century Massachusetts or other early American settlements. The fact that they may have been dressed like the same-sexed parents from about age six on is often used to support the "miniature adult" position, but may have been a way of encouraging them to identify with the parent's role and responsibilities for their future. We certainly see even toddlers today trying to mimic a parent's walk or action in order to identify with the parent.

- *Are there any strong messages about parenting then and today?*

Apart from parents' own experiences as children, there are other influences on their child-rearing practices. One such factor is whether this is the first child who has all their attention and with whom they are more likely to make mistakes, or a later child who has to share their attention with siblings, but who also profits (one hopes) from what they learned in raising the oldest. A second factor has to do with the times in which one grew up. In the 20th century, for example, if you were a child during the Depression you were doubtless taught values that differed from those taught by parents in better economic times; if your parent was in World War II, values differed from those whose young adulthood occurred during the Viet Nam war and its socio-political side effects. In Puritan times, these factors were equally potent in shaping child-rearing practices.

Consistency between parents in their views of appropriate behavior was and is critical. In the Puritan family, the wife was considered to be subordinate to her husband, so the consistency of expectations regarding children's behavior may have been greater then than now. In today's families, however, when the mother says to the erring child, "Wait until I tell your father what you've done," we are aware that the delay in dealing with the misbehavior is ineffective in correcting it and conveys mixed messages to the child about the parents' respective "power" and responsibilities.

What was perceived as acceptable discipline in the case of *mis*behavior then would be viewed in some instances as child abuse today, although even then the 1641 Code forbade excessive corporal punishment of children. The idea that "Might makes right" was not a good one then or now, but was, in fact, typical of most communities in Europe and the Americas until fairly recent times.

Parents are, or should be, responsible, however, for helping their children to become sensitive to their own needs and those of others, to develop values and a sense of personal ethics. That was done by Puritan parents within the scope of accepted church doctrine. These values systems need not be tied to a specific church or written religious explication, for no denomination has exclusive title to what is right and wrong. One person's behavior toward another should not be dependent on any specific religious faith, but rather on a more universally accepted view of what is moral and ethical, for we interact today with peoples from all over the world as well as those in our own communities.

- *What are the comparisons of self-confidence and self-esteem today versus those of the Puritan children?*

Self-esteem -- or pride in oneself -- would have been seen as sinful in Puritan times, as is still the rule in some religious denominations (e.g. the Amish). Today, on the other hand, we seek to boost a child's self-esteem so that he/she can achieve in school and later as an adult. Children are aware even before first grade how their "performance" in activities compares with that of their peers, with those seeing themselves as less able having lower self-esteem which itself often leads to lowered performance in a vicious circle. This is tied strongly to Erikson's "latency" stage (ages 7-11 years: "industry vs. inferiority").

Self-confidence will vary by age, stage of development, situation, and individual experiences –true then and now, although *then* exhibiting self-confidence might have had to

185

be in a lower key than today. A child was not be to be seen as bragging, and this is still regarded as unseemly behavior. On the other hand, most parents today try to help the child learn so that he or she can say proudly –"I can do it all by myself!" As they gain self-confidence, this contributes to positive self-esteem.

- *What were the long-term mental health issues of growing up Puritan?*

Leverenz (1980), as noted in Chapter 13, asserted that "Puritans sought, with varying degrees of success, to remold themselves into what we would now call an "obsessive-compulsive" personality..." p. 2). In many cases they succeeded. Individuals also suffered from other mental illnesses. In the case of Hugh Peter, an energetic and orthodox Puritan, for example, Leverenz says that "Like so many other Puritans, his outward contentiousness at times masked severe depression..."(p.67). Peter's wife "went insane," though no further description is given. Some of the emotional conflicts and disorders were apparently worked out in religious zeal. Those who were referred to as guilty sinners or unworthy "fountains of sin" might even become paranoid (Cable, 1975). The proportion of Puritans who became what we would consider mentally ill is really unknown, but the stresses of Colonial life, the higher mortality rate four centuries ago, the harshness of being surrounded by constant references to sin, the Devil, and the need to follow a very straight and narrow path, might well have been more than some Puritans could handle. The ones who would have been considered "crazy" would have been the non-conformists, the rebels in the family and in the town, but their symptoms might not provoke the same label today.

One of the earliest recorded references to public care for people with mental illness in America is attributed to Roger Williams, the Puritan leader of Providence, R.I. In late 1650, he urged the town council to provide for the care of a "distracted woman" (Street, 1994). She may have been "distracted" because of an inability to cope with the many demands on her time with respect to domestic responsibilities, or overwhelmed with grief because of the death of her husband, or even a child. There is simply not enough accurate data to make a definitive statement.

- *What was the role of education in Puritan times as compared with the present?*

Then, as now, mother was the child's first teacher, and "dame schools" perhaps resembled one of today's small nursery school settings. ABC's and basic reading skills were taught as well as arithmetic, religion, and cooking and sewing for the girls and more religious-oriented reading for the boys. The texts used included the *Bible*, the *Horn Book,* the *New England Primer*, and classics. The two Education acts, the first passed in 1642 requiring compulsory education for religious purposes, and the second, the "Ould Deluder Satan" Act of 1647, were focused on literacy so that all might read the Bible for themselves, to protect themselves from a negative predestination and from the world's corrupting influences. Children were also taught writing, arithmetic and other subjects in the "core curriculum" so that children would have the skills necessary for adult functioning (Schwartz, 1969).

Some communities had Latin grammar schools that prepared boys (ages 8-16) for entrance to Harvard or Yale where they might study for the ministry. However, there are ample notations in the literature that at least some boys graduated from Harvard by the age of 16, another testimony to the intellectual precocity that is alleged to have prevailed (Kaestle & Vinovskis, 1978; Kett, 1978). Kaestle and Vinovskis (1978) asserted, from their reading of Puritan history, that in the Puritan "conception of children below the age of six or seven [they were seen as] capable of more extensive intellectual development than we see in young children today...Children often learned to read at three and four, and some even received training in Latin and Greek at five and six" (p. S46). This is truly remarkable precocity if more than a few children could be so taught, especially among the general population of trades people and farmers. On the other hand, Cotton Mather, son and grandson of leading pastors in the Massachusetts Bay Colony, "showed intellectual prowess, mastering Latin, Greek, and Hebrew as a child and graduating from Harvard at the tender age of 15." (Harper, 1994, p. 21). In general, though, one must question whether their reading was mere rote learning or whether they actually comprehended what they read, with the first being the more likely for most children.

- *Corporal punishment and the 1st Amendment re religion vs. family privacy*

To the Puritans,

> proper love meant, first of all, proper discipline. Puritans and Anglicans alike looked to the family to stabilize a society in the midst of crisis and change...In a society essentially without police, the family was the basic instrument for supervision. But the concern was also spiritual. A breakdown in family rule indicates a dereliction of God's order. Rebellious children meant sinful parents (Leverenz, 1980, p. 71).

Given the cramped living quarters for each family, firm discipline had to be exercised to maintain domestic tranquility. In childhood, it was imposed; later, it was self-discipline. As part of the marital division of labor, "The mother was expected to be loving, even too loving, to the very young child. When the child reached the age of instruction, before nine or ten, the father's more distant governance was expected to check the mother's tenderness and slowly bring the child to God's authority" (Leverenz, 1980, p. 72). This did not necessarily mean corporal punishment then anymore than it does today, although beatings and whippings were common facts of life in England and elsewhere and had been for centuries. "Children learned the behavior appropriate to their sex and station by sharing the activities of their parents" (Demos, 2000, p. 140). In a sense, even today children learn behaviors by observing, if not sharing, the activities of their parents—for better or for worse. The parents' role then and now is to guide the child toward appropriate behaviors.

In the Massachusetts Bay Colony's "Body of Liberties" legislation of 1641, items #80 and #83 protect women and children from excessive bodily harm. If beaten too severely, they could complain to the civil authorities for redress. According to Somerville (1992) moreover,

> it would seem that only Puritan authors reminded their readers that the child's obedience to God overrode that due the parents, and for this reason they expressed inhibitions in all of their child-rearing manuals against the casual brutality toward children which was common in English society. Puritans wanted their children to offer obedience freely, without compulsion.

No doubt some parents harbored a lingering temptation toward compulsion, but there is not reason to believe that this amounted to a disciplinarian paranoia (p.29).

In one case described by Ulrich (1982), the father was fined for "cruel and excessive beating of his daughter" (p. 197). This was a situation reflecting individual differences, for the girl is described as being "unlike other children in the family," in that she first responded to her father's whippings with open defiance, which enraged him, which led her to resist more rather than obey, "until he had finally passed the line drawn in this society between godly sternness and cruelty" (pp.197-198).

Corporal punishment and strong shaming are still practiced in some families, because that is the only way the parents know to try to alter their children's behavior. It is the childrearing that *they* experienced, and is, in some cases, a dictate of their religion. Harsh physical discipline in childhood and youth, however, has been found to be directly related to greater use of violence against an intimate partner in later years (Swinford, DeMaris, Cernkovich, & Giordano, 2000). In some families, especially among members of some fundamentalist sects, corporal punishment is used as it was in earlier times—to control the child, to make the child fear worse punishment in Hell if the behavior did not change, not make the child ashamed and obedient.

Today, of course, corporal punishment is viewed as child abuse and is against the law. It poses conflicts between the 1st Amendment's freedom of religion clause, as well as rights to privacy of the family, and civil legislation defining child abuse. There are concerns, for example, about the discipline meted out by some religious groups in the unregulated boarding homes and day care centers that they operate, discipline that clearly violates laws against child abuse (Belluck, 2001). In cases where parents have denied medical care to a child, often resulting in the child's death, because of religious belief, the courts in recent years have begun to rule against the parents as they stress the child's best interest.

But most of the Puritans then and psychologists today recognize that parental behavior serves as a model for children's behavior. Although psychologists try to show the error of spanking children to make them behave, there are still both groups and individual families that do this. Spanking the child to beat the badness out of him (or her) follows the views of Puritans and others, but does not necessarily accomplish that goal. If anything, it may alienate child from parent, or turn the child into a confirmed rebel who is determined to do "his own thing" rather than obey someone who beats him. On the other hand, there are controversies today about "spoiling" children by allowing them to act pretty much as they will vs. being too demanding of them, although the definitions of "spoiling" and "being too demanding" depend very much on who is defining these terms.

- *Comparison with some sects, cults, extremist religious groups*

Finally, thinking of various practices with the Massachusetts Bay Colony, it was noted that some readers might perceive elements of a religious cult, at least in the first and second generations of Puritans in the Colony. Let us examine several of these elements, using two recognized denominations (Lubavitcher Chassidim and the Amish), a major religion (Roman Catholicism), and three groups regarded by much of society as modern-day cults (Unification Church, Church of Scientology, and Children of God).

As seen in the chart below, the Puritans more closely resemble the recognized religious groups than they do those considered to be cults.

Comparison of Religious Groups

	Lubavitcher Chassidim	Amish	Roman Catholic	Puritan	Unification Church	Church of Scientology	Children of God
Charismatic Leader					X	X	
Submission to Authority	X	X	X		X	X	X
Communal Lifestyle					X	X	X
Rigid Ideology	X	X	X	X	X	X	X
Restricted Communications				X	X	X*	
Isolation from Family		**			X	X	
Active Recruiting			X		X	X	X
Physiologic Deprivation					X	X	X
Hate/Fear of Outsiders					X	X	X
Assets Turned Over to Group	Tithe	Tithe	Contrib.	Contrib.	X	X	X

* - True for members living within the group's community, but not for all members.

** - The Amish practice "shunning" or separation from the community (including the family) when an individual violates the principles of their Church. This is an extreme measure, and is not a condition of membership.

The ways in which the Puritans differ from cults can be clearly seen. We know from earlier pages that families were able to (and did) practice modifications of church preachings within the privacy of their own homes. The husband/father was the authority figure within the family, not a charismatic leader. Conformity to church/communal doctrines was required, but Puritans were not as totally indoctrinated as recruits to cults have been. They were not monitored 24 hours a day as cult recruits are, so they could have independent thoughts. The Puritans, like the Amish, had preachers who conveyed the word of God, but were truly preachers rather than charismatic leaders, and they worked with the church Elders to determine what to preach. Conformity to Biblical injunctions and to community laws was certainly necessary to maintain one's acceptance within the community, but expulsion from the community for non-conformity or non-belief was not always as extreme as even that practiced by the Old Order Amish and some other sects or denominations. Corporal punishment, or physical abuse, was practiced among the Puritans for some crimes, but not for all behaviors that strayed from the straight and narrow ideology. In addition, both wives and children were protected from severe physical abuse by the 1641 Code of Liberties and other laws. This was not true among cults, where excessive physical punishment for "transgressions," often ordered by the cult leaders, could not be appealed to someone outside the "family."

In Conclusion...

In conclusion, what can be said about the Puritan children being "in exile?" Literally they were in exile from the "mother country" in order to practice their religion as they saw fit, and each succeeding generation was clearly more remote from the history and society of England. The first generation of children born in the Massachusetts Bay Colony may also have been more remote from other influences because of the distances between towns, but, again that changed as the years passed. They were in exile, if you want to consider it this way, from the rigid rule of primogeniture because there was both more space in the immediate community and the frontier beyond it, allowing for more children to inherit from the father if he had an estate to leave them, or to find a new path for themselves. As the decades passed, they became more remote, more "exiled" if you prefer, from the literal dictates of the Bible, and a bit more flexible in family life, child-rearing, and relationships with other Colonial communities, as religious leaders moved from strictly literal interpretations of Scripture to attempts to explain and justify the Lord's commands to their parishioners. Much of their philosophy, modified by time and place, can still be found in American values as transmitted by a variety of religions.

Children were not exiled from their families, although they were often sent to live with another family during their years of apprenticeship. When that was completed, they returned home and lived with their parents until they were married, and sometimes longer. As adults, they established new bonds with their parents and siblings, based on common heritage and beliefs for the most part. The tradition of putting young children to work was seen even into the nineteenth century with youngsters of eight to ten working in the New England mills, and those in the middle teens hard at work in factories and elsewhere in the twentieth century until the compulsory education law continued school above fourteen years of age.

No one can say that life was easy for Puritan children almost 400 years ago. They were raised strictly, had less recreation than our children have today, ran more health risks, and had a relatively short childhood. In this, however, they were not too different from the other children of their time whose parents followed other religious doctrines. To make too broad generalizations about the harm done by Puritan child-rearing techniques as if they were unique would be an error, for intolerance and firmness were typical of most of the colonials of that period. However, as the subsequent generations of Puritan children became aware of alternative points of view in the expanding Colonies, some of them moved away from the harsh child-rearing and religious preachings to a more moderate perspective, exiling themselves from the past to some degree.

APPENDIX

Catechism
by Reverend John Cotton
(public domain material)

Question: What is the chief end of man?
Answer: Man's chief end is to glorify God and enjoy him forever.

What rule hath God given to direct us how we may glorify and enjoy him?
The word of God, which is contained in the scriptures of the old and new testament, is the only rule to direct us how we may glorify God and enjoy him.

What do the scriptures principally teach?
The scriptures principally teach what man is to believe concerning God, and what duty God requireth of man.

What is God?
God is a spirit, infinite, eternal, and unchangeable, in his being, wisdom, power, holiness, justice, goodness, and truth.

Are there more Gods than one?
There is but ONE only, the living and true GOD.

How many persons are there in the God-head?
There are three persons in the God-head, the Father, the Son, and the Holy Ghost, and these three are one GOD, the same in substance, equal in power and glory.

What are the decrees of God?

The decrees of God are his eternal purpose, according to the counsel of his own will, whereby for his own glory he hath fore-ordained whatsoever comes to pass.

How does God execute his decrees?

God executes his decrees in the works of creation and providence.

What is the work of creation?

The work of creation is God's making all things of nothing by the word of his power, in the space of six days, and all very good.

How did God create man?

God created man male and female after his own image, in knowledge, righteousness and holiness, with dominion over the creatures.

What are God's works of providence?

God's works of providence are his most holy, wise, and powerful, preserving and governing all his creatures and all their actions.

What special act of providence did God exercise towards man in the estate wherein he was created?

When God had created man, he entered into a covenant of life with him upon condition of perfect obedience, forbidding him to eat of the tree of knowledge of good and evil, upon pain of death.

Did our first parents continue in the estate wherein they were created?
Our first parents being left to the freedom of their own will, fell from the estate wherein they were created, by sinning against God.

What is sin?
Sin is any want of conformity unto, or transgression of the law of God.

What was the sin whereby our first parents fell from the estate wherein they were created?
The sin whereby our first parents fell from the estate wherein they were created, was their eating the forbidden fruit.

Did all mankind fall in Adam's first transgression?
The covenant being made with Adam, not only for himself, but for his posterity, all mankind descending from him by ordinary generation, sinned in him, and fell with him in his first transgression.

Into what estate did the fall bring mankind?
The fall brought mankind into an estate of sin and misery.

Wherein consists the sinfulness of that estate where into man fell?
The sinfulness of that estate where into man fell, consists in the GUILT of Adam's first sin, the want of original righteousness, and the corruption of his whole nature, which is commonly called original sin (see described elsewhere), *together with all actual transgressions which proceed from it.*

What is the misery of that estate where into man fell?

All mankind by the fall lost communion with God, are under his wrath and curse, and so made liable to the miseries in this life, to death itself, and to the pains of hell forever.

Did God leave all mankind to perish in the state of sin and misery?

God having out of his mere good pleasure from all eternity ELECTED SOME to everlasting life, did enter into a covenant of grace, to deliver them out of a state of sin and misery, and to bring them into a state of salvation by a Redeemer.

Who is the Redeemer of God's ELECT?

The only Redeemer of God's elect, is the Lord Jesus Christ, who being the eternal Son of God, became man, and so was, and continues to be God and Man, in two distinct natures, and one person forever.

How did Christ being the Son of God become man?

Christ the Son of God became man by taking to himself a true body and a reasonable soul, being conceived by the power of the Holy Ghost, in the womb of the virgin Mary, and born of her, and yet without sin.

What offices does Christ execute as our Redeemer?

Christ as our Redeemer executes the office of a prophet, of a priest, and of a king, both in his estate of humiliation and exaltation.

How does Christ execute the office of a prophet?

Christ executes the office of a prophet in revealing to us by his word and spirit, the will of God for our salvation.

How does Christ execute the office of a priest?
Christ executes the office of a priest in his once offering up himself a sacrifice to satisfy divine justice, and reconcile us to God, and in making continual intercession for us.

How does Christ execute the office of a king?
Christ executes the office of a king in subduing us to himself, in ruling and defending us, and in restraining and conquering all his and our enemies.

Wherein did Christ's humiliation consist?
Christ's humiliation consisted in his being born and that in a low condition, made under the law, undergoing the miseries of this life, the wrath of God, and the cursed death of the cross, in being buried and continuing under the power of death for a time.

Wherein consists Christ's exaltation?
Christ's exaltation consist in his rising again from the dead on the third day, in ascending up into heaven, and sitting at the right hand of God the Father, and in coming to judge the world at the last day.

How are we made partakers of the redemption purchased by Christ?
We are made partakers of the redemption purchased by Christ by the effectual application of it to us by his Holy Spirit.

What is effectual calling?
Effectual calling is the work of God's Spirit, whereby convincing us of our sin and misery, enlightening our minds in the knowledge of Christ, and renewing our wills, he doth persuade and enable us to embrace Jesus Christ, freely offered to us in the gospel.

What benefits do they that are effectually called partake of in this life?

They that are effectually called do in this partake of justification, adoption, and sanctification, and the several benefits, which in this life do either accompany or flow from them.

What is justification?

Justification is an act of God's free grace, wherein he pardons all our sins, and accepts us as righteous in his sight only for the righteousness of Christ imputed to us, and received by faith alone.

What is adoption?

Adoption is an act of God's free grace, whereby we are received into the number, and have a right to all the privileges of the sons of God.

What is sanctification?

Sanctification is the work of God's free grace, whereby we are renewed in the whole man, after the image of God, and are enabled more and more to die unto sin, and live unto righteousness.

What are the benefits which in this life do accompany or flow from justification, adoption, and sanctification?

The benefits, which in this life do accompany or flow from justification, adoption and sanctification, are assurance of God's love, peace of conscience, joy in the Holy Ghost, increase of grace, and perseverance therein to the end.

What benefits do believers receive from Christ at the death?

The souls of believers are at their death made perfect in holiness, and do immediately pass into glory, and their bodies being still united to Christ do rest in the graves until the resurrection.

What benefits do believers receive from Christ at the resurrection?
At the resurrection believers being raised up to glory, shall be openly acknowledged and acquitted in the day of judgment, and made perfectly blessed in the full enjoyment of God to all eternity.

What is the duty which God requires of man?
The duty, which God requires of man, is obedience to his revealed will.

What did God at first reveal to man for the rule of his obedience?
The rule, which God at first revealed to man for his obedience was the moral law.

Where is the moral law summarily comprehended?
The moral law is summarily comprehended in the ten commandments.

What is the sum of the ten commandments?
The sum of the ten commandments is, to love the Lord our God with all our heart, with all our soul, with all our strength, and with all our mind, and our neighbour as ourselves.

What is the preface to the ten commandments?
The preface to the ten commandments is in these words, I am the Lord thy God which have brought thee out of the land of Egypt, and out of the house of bondage.

What does the preface to the ten commandments teach us?
The preface to the ten commandments teaches us, that because God is the Lord, and our God and Redeemer, therefore we are bound to keep all his commandments.

Which is the first commandment?
The first commandment is, Thou shalt have no other Gods before me.

What is required in the first commandment?
The first commandment requires us to know and acknowledge God, to be the only true God, and our God, and to worship and glorify him accordingly.

What is forbidden in the first commandment?
The first commandment forbids the denying or not worshipping and glorifying the true God, as God, and our God, and the giving that worship and glory to any other which is due to him alone.

What are we especially taught by these words in the first commandment?
These words in the first commandment, teach us, that God who seeth all things, taketh notice of and is much displeased with the sin of having any other God.

Which is the second commandment?
The second commandment is, Thou shalt not make unto thee any graven image, or the likeness of any thing that is in heaven above, or that is in the earth beneath, or that is in the water under the earth: thou shalt not bow down thyself to them nor serve them, for I the Lord thy God am a jealous God, visiting the iniquities of the fathers upon the children, unto the third and fourth generation of them that hate me

and showing mercy until thousands of them that love me and keep my commandments.

What is required in the second commandment?
The second commandment requires the receiving, observing, and keeping pure and entire all such religious worship and ordinances, as God has appointed in his word.

What is forbidden in the second commandment?
The second commandment forbids the worshipping of God by images or any other way not appointed in his word.

What are the reasons annexed to the second commandment?
The reasons annexed to the second commandment, are God's sovereignty over us, his propriety in us, and the zeal he hath to his own worship.

Which is the third commandment?
The third commandment is, Thou shalt not take the name of the Lord thy God in vain, for the Lord will not hold him guiltless that taketh his name in vain.

What is required in the third commandment?
The third commandment requires the holy and reverent use of God's names, titles, attributes, ordinances, word and works.

What is forbidden in the third commandment?
The third commandment forbids all profaning or abusing of any thing whereby God makes himself known.

What is the reason annexed to the third commandment?
The reason annexed to the third commandment is, that however the breakers of this commandment may escape

punishment from men, yet the Lord our God will not suffer them to escape his righteous judgment.

Which is the fourth commandment?
The fourth commandment is, Remember the Sabbath day to keep it holy, six days shalt thou labor and do all thy work, but the seventh day is the Sabbath of the Lord thy God, in it thou shalt not do any work, thou nor thy son, nor thy daughter, they man-servant, nor thy mail servant, nor the cattle, nor the stranger that is within thy gates, for in six days the Lord made heaven and earth, the sea and all that in them is, and rested the seventh day, wherefore the Lord blessed the Sabbath day and hallowed it.

What is required in the fourth commandment?
The fourth commandment requires, the keeping holy to God such set times as he hath appointed in his word, expressly one whole day in seven to be an holy Sabbath to himself.

Which day of the seven hath God appointed to be the weekly Sabbath?
From the beginning of the world, to the resurrection of Christ, God appointed the seventh day of the week to be the weekly Sabbath, and the first day of the week ever since to continue to the end of the world, which is the Christian Sabbath.

How is the Sabbath to be sanctified?
The Sabbath is to be sanctified by an holy resting all that day, even from such worldly employments and recreations as are lawful on other days, and spending the whole time in public and private exercises of God's worship, except so much as is to be taken up in the works of necessity and mercy.

What is the forbidden in the fourth commandment?
The fourth commandment forbids, the omission or careless performance of the duties required, and the profaning the day by idleness, or doing that which is in itself sinful, or by unnecessary thoughts, words, or works, about worldly employments or recreations.

What are the reasons annexed to the fourth commandment?
The reasons annexed to the fourth commandment, are God's allowing us six days of the week for our own employment, his challenging a special propriety in the seventh, his own example and his blessing the Sabbath day.

Which is the fifth commandment?
The fifth commandment is Honor thy father and thy mother, that thy days may be long upon the land which the Lord thy God giveth thee.

What is required in the fifth commandment?
The fifth commandment requires the preserving the honor, and performing the duties belonging to every one in their several places and relations, as superiors, inferiors, or equals.

What is forbidden in the fifth commandment?
The fifth commandment forbids the neglecting of, or doing any thing again the honour and duty which belongs to every one in their several places and relations.

What is the reason annexed to the fifth commandment?
The reason annexed to the fifth commandment is a promise of long life and prosperity to all such as keep this commandment.

Which is the sixth commandment?
The sixth commandment is, Thou shalt not kill.

What is required in the sixth commandment?
The sixth commandment requireth all lawful endeavors to preserve our own life, and the life of others.

What is forbidden in the sixth commandment?
The sixth commandment forbids the taking away of our own life, or the life or our neighbor unjustly, and whatsoever tends thereunto.

Which is the seventh commandment?
The seventh commandment is, Thou shalt not commit adultery.

What is required in the seventh commandment?
The seventh commandment requires the preservation of our own and our neighbor's chastity, in heart, speech, and behaviour.

What is forbidden in the seventh commandment?
The seventh commandment forbids all unchaste thoughts, words, and actions.

What is the eighth commandment?
The eighth commandment is, Thou shalt not steal.

What is required in the eighth commandment?
The eighth commandment requires the lawful procuring and furthering the wealth and outward estate of ourselves and others.

What is forbidden in the eighth commandment?
The eighth commandment forbiddeth whatsoever doth, or may unjustly hinder our own or our neighbour's wealth or outward estate.

What is the ninth commandment?
The ninth commandment is, Thou shalt not bear false witness against thy neighbour.

What is required in the ninth commandment?
The ninth commandment requires the maintaining and promoting of truth between man and man, and of our own and our neighbour's good name, especially in witness bearing.

What is forbidden in the ninth commandment?
The ninth commandment forbids whatsoever is prejudicial to truth, or injurious to our own or our neighbour's good name.

Which is the tenth commandment?
The tenth commandment is, Thou shalt not covet thy neighbour's house, thou shalt not covet thy neighbour's wife, nor his man-servant, nor his maid-servant, nor his ox, nor his ass, nor anything that is thy neighbour's.

What is required in the tenth commandment?
The tenth commandment requires full contentment with our own condition, with a right and charitable frame of spirit towards our neighbor, and all that is his.

What is forbidden in the tenth commandment?
The tenth commandment forbids all discontentment with our own estate, envying or grieving at the good of our neighbour, and all inordinate motions and affections to anything that is his.

Is man able perfectly to keep the commandments of God?

No mere man since the fall is able in this life perfectly to keep the commandments of God, but daily breaks them in though, word and deed.

Are all transgressions of the law equally heinous?

Some sins in themselves, and by reason of several aggravations, are more heinous in the sight of God than others.

What does every sin deserve?

Every sin deserves God's wrath and curse both in this life, and that which is to come.

What does God require of us that we may escape his wrath and curse due to us for sin?

To escape the wrath and curse of God due to us for sin, God requires of us faith in Jesus Christ, repentance unto life, with the diligent use of all outward means whereby Christ communicates to us the benefits of redemption.

What is faith in Jesus Christ?

Faith in Jesus Christ is a saving grace whereby we receive and rest upon him alone for salvation as he is offered to us in the gospel.

What is repentance unto life?

Repentance unto life is a saving grace, whereby a sinner out of the true sense of his son an apprehension of the mercy of God in Christ, does with grief and hatred of his sin turn from it unto God, with full purpose of and endeavors after new obedience.

What are the outward and ordinary means whereby Christ communicates to us the benefits of redemption?
The outward and ordinary means whereby Christ communicates to us the benefits of redemption, are his ordinances, especially the word, sacraments and prayer; all which are made effectual to the elect for salvation.

How is the word made effectual to salvation?
The spirit of God makes the reading, but especially the preaching of the word an effectual means of convincing and converting sinners, and of building them up in holiness and comfort, through faith unto salvation.

How is the word to be read and heard that it may become effectual to salvation?
That the word may become effectual to salvation, we must attend thereunto with diligence, preparation and prayer, receive it with faith and love, lay it up in our hearts, and practice it in our lives.

How do the sacraments become effectual means of salvation?
The sacraments become effectual means of salvation not from any virtue in them or in him that administers them, but only by the blessing of Christ, and the working of the Spirit in them that by faith receive them.

What is a sacrament?
A sacrament is a holy ordinance instituted by Christ, wherein by sensible signs, Christ and the benefits of the new covenant are represented sealed and applied to believers.

What are the sacraments of the New Testament?
The sacraments of the New Testament are baptism and the Lord's supper.

What is baptism?

Baptism is a sacrament wherein the washing of water in the name of the Father and of the Son and of the Holy Ghost, doth signify and seal our ingrafting into Christ and partaking of the benefits of the covenant of grace, and our engagements to be the Lord's.

To whom is baptism to be administered?

Baptism is not be administered to any that are out of the visible church, till they profess their faith in Christ, and obedience to him, but the infants of such as are members of the visible church are to be baptized.

What is the Lord's Supper?

The Lord's supper is a sacrament, wherein by giving and receiving bread and wine according to Christ's appointment, his death is showed forth, and the worthy receivers are not after a corporal and carnal manner, but by faith made partakers of his body and blood with all his benefits, to their spiritual nourishment and growth in grace.

What is required in the worthy receiving the Lord's supper?

It is required of them that would worthily partake of the Lord's supper, that they examine themselves of their knowledge to discern the Lord's body, of their faith to feed upon him, of their repentance, love and new obedience, lest coming unworthily, they eat and drink judgment to themselves.

What is prayer?

Prayer is an offering up of our desires to God for things agreeable to his will, in the name of Christ, with confession of our sins, and thankful acknowledgment of his mercies.

What rule hath God given for our direction in prayer?
The whole word of God is of use to direct us in prayer but the special rule of direction is that form of prayer, which Christ taught his disciples commonly called, The Lord's Prayer.

What does the preface of the Lord's prayer teach us?
*The preface of the Lord's prayer which is **Our Father which art in Heaven,** teaches us, to draw near to God with all holy reverence and confidence, as children to a father, able and ready to help us, and that we should pray with and for others.*

What do we pray for in the first petition?
*In the first petition, which is **Hallowed be thy name**, we pray that God would enable us and others to glorify him in all that whereby he makes himself known, and that he would dispose all things to his own glory.*

What do we pray for in the second petition?
*In the second petition, which is, **Thy kingdom come**, we pray that Satan's kingdom may be destroyed, the kingdom of grace may be advanced, ourselves and others brought into it, and kept in it, and that the kingdom of glory may be hastened.*

What do we pray for in the third petition?
*In the third petition, which is, **Thy will be done on earth as it is in heaven**, we pray that God by his grace would make us able and willing to know, obey and submit to his will in all things, as the angels do in heaven.*

What do we pray for in the fourth petition?
*In the fourth petition, which is, **Give us this day our daily bread**, we pray that of God's free gift we may receive a*

competent portion of the good things of this life, and enjoy his blessing with them.

What do we pray for in the fifth petition?
In the fifth petition, which is, **And forgive us our debts as we forgive our debtors**, *we pray that God for Christ's sake, would freely pardon all our sins, which we are the rather encouraged to ask, because by his grace we are enabled from the heart to forgive others.*

What do we pray for in the sixth petition?
In the sixth petition, which is, **And lead us not into temptation**, *but deliver us from evil, we pray that God would either keep us from being tempted to sin, or support and deliver us when we are tempted.*

What doest the conclusion of the Lord's prayer teach us?
The conclusion of the Lord's prayer, which is, **For thine is the kingdom, and the power, and the glory, forever, AMEN**, *teaches us, to take our encouragement in prayer from God only, and in our prayers to praise him, ascribing kingdom, power and glory to him, and in testimony of our desire and assurance to be heard, we say, AMEN.*

Spiritual Milk for Babes Drawn out of the Breasts of both Testaments for their Souls Nourishment
By [Reverend] John Cotton
(public domain material)

What hath God done for you?
God hath made me, he keepeth me, and he can save me.

What is God?
God is a Spirit of himself and for himself.

How many Gods are there?
There is but one God in three Persons, the Father, and the Son, and the Holy Ghost.

How did God make you?
In my first parents [Adam and Eve] holy and righteous

Are you then born holy and righteous?
No, my first father sinned and I in him.

What is your birth sin?
Adam's sin imputed to me, and a corrupt nature dwelling in me.

What is your corrupt nature?
My corrupt nature is empty of grace, bent unto sin, only unto sin, and that continually.

What is sin?
Sin is a transgression of the law.

How many commandments of the law be there?
Ten

What is the first commandment?
You shall have no other Gods before me.
What is the meaning of this commandment?
We should worship the only true God, and no other.

What is the second commandment?
You shall not make to yourself any graven image.

What is the meaning of this commandment?
That we should worship the only true God, with true worship, such as he has ordained, not such as man has invented.

What is meant by the name of God?
God himself and the good things of God, whereby he is known as a man by his name, and his attributes, worship, word, and works.

What is it not to take his name in vain?
To make use of God & the good things of God to his glory, and our own good, not vainly, not irreverently, not unprofitably.

Which is the fourth commandment?
Remember that you keep holy the Sabbath day.

What is the meaning of this commandment?
That we should rest from labor, and much more from play on the Lord's day, that we may draw nigh to God in holy duties.

What is the fifth commandment?
Honor your father and thy mother, that your days may be long in the land which the Lord you God gives you.

What are meant by father and mother?
All our superiors whether in family, school, church, and commonwealth.

What is the honor due unto them?
Reverence, obedience, and recompence.

What is the sixth commandment?
Thou shalt do no murder.

What is the meaning of this commandment?
That we should not shorten the life or health of ourselves or others, but preserve both.

What is the sin here forbidden?
To defile ourselves or others with unclean lusts.

What is the duty here commanded?
Chastity to possess our vessel in holiness and honor.

What is the eighth commandment?
That shalt not steal.

What stealing is here forbidden?
To take away another man's goods without his leave, or to spend our own without benefit to ourselves or other.

What is the duty here commanded?
To get our goods honestly, to keep them safely, and spend them thriftly.

What is the ninth commandment?
You shall not bear false witness against your neighbor.

What is the sin here forbidden?
To lie falsely, to think or speak untruly of ourselves or others.

What is the duty here required?
Truth and faithfulness.

What is the tenth commandment?
You shall not covet.

What is the coveting here forbidden?
Lust after the things of other men, and want of contentment with our own.

Have you kept all these commandments?
No, I and all men are sinners.

What are the wages of sin?
Death and damnation.

How can you be saved?
Only by Jesus Christ.

Who is Jesus Christ?
The eternal Son of God, who for our sakes became man, that he might redeem and save us.

How does Christ redeem and save us?
By his righteous life, and bitter death, and glorious resurrection to life again.

How do we come to have a part and fellowship with Christ in his death and resurrection?
By the power of his word and spirit, which brings us to him, and keeps us in him.

What is the word?
The Holy Scriptures of the prophets and apostles, the old and new testament the law and gospel.

How does the ministry of the law bring you toward Christ?
By bringing me to know my sin, and the wrath of God, against me for it.

What are you hereby the nearer to Christ?
So I come to feel my cursed estate and need of a Saviour.

How does the ministry of the Gospel help you in this cursed estate?
By humbling me yet more, and then raising me out of this estate.

How does the ministry of the Gospel humble you yet more?
By revealing the grace of the Lord Jesus in dying to save sinners, and yet convincing me of my sin in not believing on him, and of my utter insufficiency to come to him and so I feel myself utterly lost.

How does the ministry of the gospel raise you up out of this lost estate to come to Christ?
By teaching me the value and virtue of the death of Christ, and the riches of his grace to lost sinners by revealing the promise of grace to such, and by ministering the Spirit of grace to apply Christ, and his promise of grace unto myself, and to keep me in him.

How does the Spirit of grace apply Christ and his promise of grace unto you and keep you in him?
By begetting in me faith to receive him, prayer to call upon him, repentance to mourn after him, and new obedience to serve him.

What is faith?
Faith is the grace of the Spirit, whereby I deny myself, and believe on Christ for righteousness and salvation.

What is prayer?
It is calling upon God in the name of Christ by the help of the Holy Ghost, according to the will of God.

What is repentance?
Repentance is a grace of the Spirit, whereby I loath my sins and myself for them and confess them before the Lord, and mourn after Christ for the pardon of them, and for grace to serve him in newness of life.

What is the newness of life, or new obedience?
Newness of life is a grace of the Spirit, whereby I forsake my former lust and vain company, and walk before the Lord in the light of his word, and in the communion of saints.

What is the communion of saints?
It is the fellowship of the Church in the blessings of the covenant of grace, and the seals thereof.

What is the church?
It is a congregation of saints joined together in the bond of the covenant, to worship the Lord, and to edify one another in all his holy ordinances.

What is the bond of the covenant by which the church is joined together.

It is the profession of that covenant which God has made with his faithful people, to be God until them, and to their seed.

What does the Lord bind his people to in this covenant?

To give up themselves and their seed first to the Lord to be his people, and then to the elders and brethren of the Church to set forward the worship of God and their mutual edification.

How do they give up themselves and their seed to the Lord?

By receiving through faith the Lord and his covenant to themselves, and to their seed and accordingly walking themselves and training up their children in the ways of the covenant.

How do they give up themselves and their seed to the elders and brethren of the church?

By confessing of their sins, and profession of their faith, and of their subjection to the gospel of Christ, and so they and their seed are received into the fellowship of the church and the seals thereof.

What are the seals of the covenant now in the days of the gospel?

Baptism and the Lord's Supper.

What is done for you in baptism?

In baptism the washing with water is a sign and seal of my washing in the blood and spirit of Christ, and thereby of my ingrafting into Christ, of the pardon and cleansing of my sins, or my raising up out of afflictions and also of my resurrection from the dead at the last day.

What is done for you in the Lord's Supper?

In the Lord's Supper, the receiving of the bread broken and the wine poured out is a sign and seal of my receiving the communion of the body of Christ broken for me and of his blood shed for me, and thereby of my growth in Christ and the pardon and healing of my sins, of the fellowship of the Spirit, of my strengthening and quickening in grace, and of my sitting together with Christ on his throne of glory at the last judgment.

What was the resurrection from the dead, which was sealed up to you in baptism?

When Christ shall come in his last judgment, all that are in their graves shall rise again, both the just and unjust.

What is the judgment which is sealed up to you in the Lord's Supper?

At the last day we shall all appear before the judgment seat of Christ, to give an account of our works, and receive our reward according to them.

What is the reward that shall then be given?

The righteous shall go into life eternal, and the wicked shall be cast into everlasting fire with the Devil and his angels.

List of Ninety Books Borrowed by Reverend Richard Mather in 1647 from Captain John Johnson
(public domain material)

____New Covenant. God's
   Allsuffic[ient]
____on Job
____on John
____on Isaiah

____on Opuscula:Ward
Sermons & Tyreatises
____Last pt of Warfare
Ferus,Enanaarationes
____Second pt of Warfare
____Third pt of Warfare
Alsted: Lexicon Theologicum
Ames: Rescriptio adversus of
Assertion of Goum
Ayry on the Phillipians
Babington's Works chap.
Bayne, Helpe to Happinesse
Beard, Theater of God's
 Judgments
Benefield: on Amos 1
Bifield on the Creed
Bradshaw on 2 Thessalonians
Bucan Institutions
Bunting Itenerarium
Bythner Manipulus Messie of
 Magnae

Evangeliorium
Dowman: Christian
 warfare
Dowman on Hosea
Elton on
 Colossians
Elton on Romans 7
Elton on Romans 8

Ferus, Exegesis
Ferus, on John
Fox Eicasmi on Rev
Gerard Conquest

 temptations
Goodwin, Synopsis
Greenhill on 5

 of Ezekiel
Gualther on Acts
Harris Works
Hofmeister on Mark
J.D. Exposition of
 Lord's Prayer
Jo: Rodgers: Doctrine of
 Faith
Lewis: Right vse

 Promises

Chemnitius Examen Concil:
Trident
Crooke Guide to True Bless-
Ednesse
Cyprian's Works
Dent on the Revelation
Dietericus Analysis Logica
Negus: Man's Active
Obedience
Culverwell
Neh: Rogers on 2 Parables
Orsinus, Explicate:
Catecheticae
Parre on Romans 8-16
Peter Martyr on Judges
Practice of Christianity
Thessalonians
Preston: Faith and Love
Preston: 4 Treatieses
2
Preston:Remaynes
Preston: Saints Qualification
Prick: Doctrine of Superior-
ity and Subjection
Prideaux: Orationos
Randall on Romans 8-33 &c.
Rich: Preston: Sacrament
ps
Rogers on Judges
Rollack de Vocatione
Efficaci
Rollack on 1 Thessalonians
Vdall: on Lamentations
Winckelman: Small Pro-
Phets

Lord Supper
Luther on Galathians
Malcolumus on Acts
Man's Uprightness
Marlorat on Esai
Moulin of Love of God
Musculus: Mathew
Salmons Sermon
Ecclesiastes

of Faith
Sedgwick: Bearing &
Burden of Spirit
Seneca his works
Sibbs: Soules Conflict
Slater on

Smyth on Hosea 6th
Stevartius Leodius in

Corinthians
Symonds: Desertions
Taylor: Parable of the
Sower
Taylor: upon Titus
Theordoricus Analys:
logica in Evangel:

Hyemalis
Topsell: on Ruth
Tossanus Pastor Evan-
gelicus
Whateley: Carecloath
Yates: Arraignement
of Hypocrites

In all 90 bookes pr. me Richard Mather

[Note: List is from the <u>Collections</u> of the Massachusetts Historical Society that include *The Mather Papers.*" Many of the surnames and titles were not spelled correctly by Richard Mather.

Richard Mather of Toxteth, England was preacher at Dorchester, MA from 1631 to 1669. This Richard Mather was the grandfather of the famous Rev. Cotton Mather who has been called "the last Puritan." Rev. John Cotton was Cotton Mather's other grandfather.

At least 55 from the above list are in three of the libraries located at Yale University, New Haven, CT. The remaining books are scattered between the Harvard University Library, Cambridge, MA, the Sutro Library, San Francisco, CA, Union Theological Seminary, New York City, NY, Avon Library in Bristol, England, and the library at Oxford University, Oxford, England, and in microform at Lewis and Clark College Law Library, Portland, OR, Hatfield Library at Willamette University, Salem, OR and the Knight Memorial Library, University of Oregon, Eugene, Oregon.

Examination of these books are instructive in regard to the type of theological information was provided for the Puritan consumer of religion. When appropriate for clarification within a chapter in this book, parts of most of the books are quoted.

In many cases, the Puritan citizens knew as much theology as the Divines or preachers [sometimes called "Teachers."] Preachers were chosen by the elders of the Churches based upon what theology was close to what the congregation knew or in some cases, needed. It was not unusual for the Puritan to have many books. Nearly all of the male Emigrant Founders could read and write.]

The Massachusetts Body of Liberties (1641)
(public domain material)

The free fruition of such liberties Immunities and priveledges as humanitie, Civilitie, and Christianitie call for as due to every man in his place and proportion without impeachment and Infringement hath ever bene and ever will be the tranquilities and Stabilitie of Churches and Commonwealths. And the denial or deprival thereof, the disturbance if not the ruine of both.

We hold it therefore our dutie and safetie whilst we are about the further establishing of this Government to collect and expresse all such freedoms as for present we foresee may concerne us, and our posteritie after us, And to ratify them with our sollemne consent.

We doe therefore this day religiously and unanimously decree and confirme these following Rites, liberties and priveledges concerneing our Churches, and Civill State to respectively impartiallie and inviolably enjoyed and observed throughout our Jurisdiction for ever.

1. No mans life shall be taken away, no mans honour or good name shall be stayned, no mans person shall be arrested, restayned, banished, dismembred, nor any wayes punished, no man shall be deprived of his wife or children, no mans goods or estaite shall be taken away from him, nor any way indammaged under colour of law or Countenance of Authoritie, unlesse it be by vertue or equitie of some expresse law of the Country warranting the same, established by a general Court and sufficiently published, or in case of the defect of a law in any parteculer case by the word of God. And in Capitall

cases, or in cases concerning dismembering or banishment according to that word to be judged by the Generall Court.

2. Every person within this Jurisdiction, whether Inhabitant or forreiner shall enjoy the same justice and law, that is general for the plantation, which we constitute and execute one towards another without partialitie or delay.

3. No man shall be urged to take any oath or subscribe any articles, covenants or remonstrance, of a publique and Civill nature, but such as the Generall Court hath considered, allowed and required.

4. No man shall be punished for not appearing at or before any Civill Assembly, Court, Councell, Magistate, or Officer, nor for the omission of any office or service, if he shall be necessarily hindred by any apparent Act or providence of God, which he could neither foresee nor avoid. Provided that this law shall not prejudice any person of his just cost or damage, in any civill action.

5. No man shall be compelled to any publique worke or service unlesse the presse be grounded upon some act of the generall Court, and have reasonable allowance therefore.

6. No man shall be pressed in person to any office, worke, warres or other publique service, that is necessarily and suffitiently exempted by any naturall or personall impediment, as by want of yeares, greatnes of age, defect of minde, fayling of sences, or importencie of Lymbes.

7. No man shall be compelled to goe out of the limits of this plantation upon any offensive warres which this Commonwealth or any of our friends or confederates

shall voluntarily undertake. But onely upon such vindictive and defensive warres in our owne behalfe or the behalfe of our friends and confereats as shall be enterprized by the Counsell and consent of a Court generall, or by authority derived from the same.

8. No mans Cattel or goods of what kind soever shall be pressed or taken for any publique use or service, unlesse it be by warrant grounded upon some act of the generall Court, nor without such reasonable prices and hire as the ordinarie rates of the Countrie do afford. And if his Cattle or goods shall perish or suffer damage in such service, the owner shall be suffitiently recompenced.

9. No monopolies shall be granted or allowed amongst us, but of such new Inventions that are profitable to the Countrie, and that for a short time.

10. All our lands and heritages shall be free from all fines and licenses upon Alienations, and from all hariotts, wardships, Liveries, Primer-seisins, yeare day and wast, Escheates, and forfeitures, upon the deaths of parents or Ancestors, be they naturall, casuall, or Juditiall.

11. All persons which are of the age of 21 yeares, and of right understanding and memories, whether excommunicate or condemned shall have full power and libertie to make there wills and testaments, and other lawfull alienations of theire lands and estates.

12. Every man whether Inhabitant or fforreiner, free or not free shall have libertie to come to any publique Court, Councel, or Towne meeting, and either by speech or writeing to move any lawfull, seasonable, and materiall question, or to present any necessary motion, complaint, petition, Bill or information, whereof that meeting hath

proper cognizance, so it be done in convenient time, due order, and respective manner.

13. No man shall be rated here for any estaite or revenue he hath in England, or in any forreine partes till it be transported hither.

14. Any conveyance or Alienation of land or other estaite what so ever, made by any woman that is married, any childe under age, Ideott or distracted person, shall be good if it be passed and ratified by the consent of a generall Court.

15. All Covenous or fraudulent Alienation of lands, tenements, or any heriditaments, shall be of no validitie to defeate any man from due debts or legacies, or from any just title, clame or possession, of that which is so fraudulently conveyed.

16. Every Inhabitant that is an howse holder shall have free fishing and fowling in any great ponds and Bayes, Coves and Rivers, so farre as the sea ebbes and flowes within the presincts of the towne where they dwell, unlesse the free men of the same Towne or the Generall Court have otherwise appropriated them, provided that this shall not be extended to give leve to any man to come upon other proprietie without there leave.

17. Every man of or within this Jurisdiction shall have free libertie, notwithstanding any Civill power to remove both himselfe, and his familie at their pleasure out of the same, provided there be no legall impediment to the contrarie.

18. No mans person shall be restained by any authority whatsoever, before the law hath sentenced him thereto, if he can put in ssufficient securitie bayle or mainprise, for his appearance, and good behaviour in the meane time, unlesse it be in Crimes Capitall, and Contempts in open Court, and in such cases where some expresse act of Court doth allow it.

19. If in a general Court any miscarriage shall be amongst the Assistants when they are by themselves that may deserve an Admonition or fine under 20 sh. It shall be examined and sentenced amongst themselves, If amongst the Deputies when they are by themselves, it shall be examined and sentenced amongst themselves, If it be withn the whole Court is together, it shall be judged by the whole Court, and not severallie as before.

20. If any which are to sit as Judges in any other Court shall demeane themselves offensively in the Court, The rest of the Judges present shall have power to censure him for it, if the cause be of a high nature it shall be presented to and censured at the next superior Court.

21. In all cases where the first summons are not served six dayes before the Court, and the cause briefly specified in the warrant, where appearance is to be made by the parite summoned, it shall be at this libertie whether he will appeare or no, except all cases that are to be handled in Courts suddainly called, upon extraordinary occasions, In all cases where there appears present and urgent cause any assistant or officer appointed shal have power to make out attaichments for the first summons.

22. No man shall be adjudged to pay for detaining any debt from any Creditor above eight pounds in the hundred for one yeare, And not above that rate proportionable for all somes what so ever, neither shall this be a coulour or countenance to allow any usurie amongst us contraire to the law of god.

23. No man in any suit or action against an other shall falsely pretend great debts or damages to vex his adversary, if it shall appeare any doth so, The Court shall have power to set a reasonable fine on his head.

24. In all Trespasses or damages done to any man or men, If it can be proved to be done by the mere default of him or them to whome the trespasse is done, It shall be judged no trespasse, nor any damage given for it.

25. No Summons pleading Judgement, or any kinde of proceeding in Court or course of Justice shall be abated, arrested or reversed upon any kinde of cercumstantiall errors or mistakes, If the person and cause be rightly understood and intended by the Court.

26. Every man that findeth himselfe unfit to plead his owne cause in any Court shall have Libertie to imploy any man against whom the Court doth not accept, to helpe him, Provided he give him noe fee or reward for his paines. This shall not exempt the partie him selfe from Answering such Questions in person as the Court shall thinke meete to demand of him.

27. If any plantife shall give into any Court a declaration of his cause in writeing, The defendant shall also have libertie and time to give in his answer in writeing, And so in all further proceedings between partie and partie, So it

doth not further hinder the dispatch of Justice then the Court shall be willing unto.

28. The plantife in all Actions brought in any Court shall have libertie to withdraw his Action, or to be nonsuited before the Jurie hath given in their verdict, in which case he shall always pay full cost and chardges to the defendant, and may afterwards renew his suite at an other Court if he please.

29. In all actions at law it shall be the libertie of the plantife and defendant by mutual consent to choose whether they will be tried by the Bensh or by a Jurie, unlesse it be where the law upon just reason hath otherwise determined. The like libertie shall be pranted to all persons in Creminall cases.

30. In shall be in the libertie both of plantife and defendant, and likewise every delinquent (to be judged by a Jurie) to challenge any of the Jurors. And if his challenge be found just and reasonable by the Bench, or the rest of the Jurie, as the challenger shall be allowed him, and tales de cercumstantibus impaneled in their room.

31. In all cases where evidences is so obscure or defective that the Jurie cannot clearly and safely give a positive verdict, in which last, tht is in a spetiall verdict, the Judgement of the cause shall be left to the Court, and all Jurors shall have libertie in matters of fact if they cannot finde the maine issue, yet to finde and present in their verdict so much as they can, If the Bench and Jurors shall so suffer at any time about their verdict that either of them cannot proceed with peace of conscience the case shall be referred to the Generall Court, who shall take the question from both and determine it.

32. Everyman shall have libertie to replevy his Cattell or goods impounded, distreined, seised, or extended, unlesse it be upon execution after Judgment, and in payment of fines. Provided he puts in good securitie to prosecute his replevin, And to satisfie such demands as his Adversary shall recover against him in Law.

33. No mans person shall be arrest, or imprisoned upon execution or judgment for any debt or fine, If the law can finde competent meanse of of satisfaction otherwise from his estaite, and if not his person may be arrested and imprisioned where he shall be kept at his owne charge, not the plantife's till satisfaction be mae, unlesse the Court that had cognizance of the cause or some superior Court shall otherwise provide.

34. If any man shall be proved and Judged a commen Barrator vexing others with unjust frequent and endlesse suites, It shall be in the power of Courts both to denie him the benefit of the law, and to punish him for his Barratry.

35. No mans corne nor hay that is in the field or upon the Cart, nor his garden stuffe, nor any thing subject to present decay, shall be taken in any distresse, unlesse he that takes it doth presently bestow it where it may not be imbesled nor suffer spoile or decay, or give securitie to satisfie the worth thereof it it comes to any harme.

36. It shall be in the libertie of everyman cast condemned or sentenced in any cause in any Inferior Court, to make their appeale to the Court of Assistants, provided they tender their appeale and put in securitie to prosecute it, before the Court be ended wherein they were condemned, And within six dayes next ensuing put in good securitie before some Assistant to satisfie what his

Adversarie shall recover against him; And if the cause be of a Criminall nature for his good behaviour, and appearance, And everie man shall have libertie to complaine to the Generall Court of any Injustice done him in any Court of Assistants or other.

37. In all cases where it appears to the Court that the palntife hath willingly and wittingly done wronge to the defendant in commenceing and prosecuting an action or complaint against him, They shall have power to impose upon him a proportionable fine to the use of the defendant or accused person, for his false complaint or clamor.

38. Everie man shall have libertie to Record in the publique Rolles of any Court any Testimony given upon oath in the same Court, or before two Assistants, or any deede or evidence legally confirmed there to remaine in perpetuam rei memoriam, that is for perpetuall memorial or evidence upon occasion.

39. In all actions both reall and personall between partie and partie, the Court shall have power to respite execution for a convenient time, when in their prudence they see just cause so to doe.

40. No Conveyance, Deede, or promise whatsoever shall be of validitie, If it be gotten by Illegal violence, imprisonment, threatening, or any kinde of forcible compulsion called Dures.

41. Everie man that is to Answere for any criminall cause, whether he be in prison or under bayle, his cause shall be heard and determined at th next Court that hath proper Cognizance thereof, And may be done without prejudice of Justice.

42. No man shall be twise sentenced by Civill Justice for one and the same Crime, offence, or Trespasse.

43. No man shall be beaten with above 40 stripes, nor shall any true gentlemen, nor any man equall to a gentlemen be punished with whipping, unless his crime be very shamefull, and his course of life vitious and profligate.

44. No man condemned to dye shall be put to death within fower dayes next after his condemnation, unless the Court see spetiall cause to the contrary, or in case of martiall law, nor shall the body of any man so put to death be unburied 12 howers unlesse it be in case of Anatomie.

45. No man shall be forced by Torture to confesse any Crime against himselfe nor any other unlesse it be in some Capitall case, where his is first fullie convicted by cleare and suffitient evidence to be guilty, After which if the cause be of that nature, That it is very apparent there be other conspiratours, or confederates with him, Then he may be tortured, yet not with such Tortures as be Barbarous and inhumane.

46. For bodilie punishments we allow amongst us none that are inhumane Barbarous or cruel.

47. No man shall be put to death without the testimony of two or thre witnesses or that which equivalent thereunto.

48. Every Inhabitant of the Countrie shall have free libertie to search and veewe any Rooles, Records, or Registers of any Court or office except the Councell, And to have a transcript or exemplification thereof written examined, and signed by the hand of the officer of the office paying the appointed fees therefore.

49. No free man shall be compelled to serve upon Juries above two Courts in a yeare, except grand Jurie men, who shall hould two Courts together at the least.

50. All Jurors shall be chosen continuallie by the freemen of the Towne where they dwell.

51. All Associates selected at any time to Assist the Assitants in Inferior Courts, shall be nominted by the Townes belonging to that Court, by orderly agreement amonge themselves.

52. Children, Idiots, Distracted persons, and all that are strangers, or new comers to our plantation, shall have such allowances and dispensations in any cause whether Criminal or other as religion and reason required.

53. The age of discretion for passing away of lands or such knde of herediments, or for giving, of votes, verdicts or Sentence in any Civill Courts or causes, shall be one and twentie yeares.

54. Whensoever any thing is to be put to vote, any sentence to be pronounced, or any other matter to be proposed, or read in any Court or Assembly, If the president or moderator thereof shall refuse to performe it, the Major parte of the members of that Court or Assembly shall have power to appoint any other meete man of them to do it, And if there be just cause to punish him that should and would not.

55. In all suites or Actions in any Court, the plaintife shall have libertie to make all the titles an claims to that he sues for he can. And the Defendant shall have libertie to plead all the pleas he can in answere to them, and the Court shall judge according to the intire evidence of all.

56. If any man shall behave himselfe offensively at any Towne meeting, the rest of the freemen then present, shall have power to sentence him for his offence. So be it the mulct or penaltie exceede not twentie shilings.

57. Whensoever any person shall come to any suddaine untimely andunnaturall death, Some assistant, or the Constables of that Towne shall forthwith summon a Jury of twelve free men to inquire of the cause and manner of their death, and shall present a true verdict thereof to some neere Assistant, or the next Cour to be helde for that Towne upon their oath.

Liberties more peculiarlie concerning the free men

58. Civil Authoritie hath power and libertie to see the peace, ordinances and Rules of Christ observed in every church according to his word, so it be done in a Civill and not in an Ecclesiatical way.

59. Civill Authoritie hath power and libertie to deale with any Church member in a way of Civill Justice, notwithstanding any Church relation, office or interest.

60. No church censure shall degrade or depose any man from any Civill dignitie, office, or Authoritie he shall have in the Commonwealth.

61. No Magestrate, Juror, Officer, or other man shall be bound to informe present or reveale any private crim or offence, wherein there is no peril or danger to this plantation or any member thereof, when any necessarie tye of conscience binds him to secresie grounded upon the word of god, unlesse it be in case of testimony lawfully required.

62. Any Shire or Towne shall have libertie to choose their Deputies whom and where they please for the Generall Court. So be it they be free men, and have taken there oath of fealtie, and Inhabiting in the Jurisdiction.

63. No Governor, Deputy Governor, Assistant, Associate, or grand Jury man at any Court, not any Deputie for the General Court, shall at any time beare his owne chardges at any Court, but their necessary expences ahll be defrayed either by the Towne or Shire on whose service they are, or by the Country in generall.

64. Everie Action betweene partie and partie, and proceedings against delinquents in Criminall causes shall be firefly and distinctly entered on the Rolles of every Court by the Recorder thereof. That such actions be not afterwards brought againe to the vexation of any man.

65. No custome or prescription shall ever prevaile amongst us in any morall cause, our meaneing is maintaine anythinge that can be proved to be morallie sinfull by the word of god.

66. The Freemen of every Towneship shall have power to make such by laws and constitutions as may concerne the welfare of their Towne, provided they be not of a Criminall, but onely of a predential nature, And that their penalties exceede not 20 sh. For one offence. And that they be not regunnant to be publique laws and orders of the Countrie. And if any Inhabitant shall neglect or refuse to observe them, they shall have power to levy the appointed penalties by distresse.

67. It is the constant libertie of the free men of this plantation to choose yearly at the Court of Election out of the freemen all the General officers of this Jurisdiction. If

they please to dischardge them at the day of Election by way of vote. They may do it without shewing cause. But if at any other generall Court, we hould it due justice, that the reasons thereof be alleadged and proved. By Generall officers we meane, our Governor, Deputy Governor, Assistants, Treasurer, Generall of our warres. And our Admirall at Sea, and such as are or hereafter may be of the like generall nature.

68. It is the libertie of the freemen to choose such deputies for the Generall Court out of themselves, either in their owne Townes or elsewhere as they judge fittest. And because we cannot foresee what varietie and weight of occasions may fall into future consideration, And what counsels we may stand in neede of, we decree. That the Deputies (to attend the Generall Court in the behalfe of the Countrie) shall not any time be stated or inacted, but from Court to Court, or at the most but for one yeare, that the Countrie may have an Annuall libertie to do in that case what is most behoofefull for the best welfaire thereof.

69. No Generall Court shall be desolved or adjourned without the consent of the Major parte thereof.

70. All Freemen called to give any advise, note, verdict, or sentence in any Court, Counsell, or Civill Assembly, shall have full freedome to doe it according to their true Judgements and Consciences, So it be done orderly and inoffensively for the manner.

71. The Governor shall have a casting voice whensoever an Equi vote shall fall out in the Court of Assistants, or generall assembly, So shall the president or moderator have in all Civill Courts or Assemblies.

72. The Governor and Deputy Governor Joyntly consenting or any three Assistants concurring in consent shall have power out of Court to reprive a condemned malefactour, till the next quarter or generall Court. The generall Court onely shall have power to pardon a condemned malefactor.

73. The Generall Court hath libertie and Authoritie to send out any member of this Comanwealth of what qualitie, conditon or office whatsoever into forreine parts about any publique message or Negotiation. Provided the partie sent be acquainted with the affaire he goeth about, and be willing to undertake the service.

74. The freemen of every Towne or Towneship, shall have full power to choose yearly or for lesse time out of themselves a convenient number of fitt men to order the planting or prudentiall occasions of that Towne, according to Instructions given them in writeing, Provided nothing be done by them contrary to the publique laws and orders of the Countrie, provided also the number of such select persons be not above nine.

75. It is and shall be the libertie of any member or members of any Court Councell or Civill Assembly in cases of making or executing any order or law, that properlie concrne religion, or any cuase capitall, or warres, or Subscription to any publique Articles or Remonstance, in case they cannot in Judgement and conscience consent to that way the Major vote or suffrage goes, to make their contra Remonstrance or protestation in speech or writeing, and upon request to have their dissent recorded in the Rolls of that Court. So it be done Christianlie and respectively for the manner. And their dissent onely be

entered without the reasons thereof, for the avoiding of tediousness.

76. Whensoever any Jurie of trialls or Jurours are not clere in their Judgments or consciences conserneing any cause wherein they are to give their verdict, They shall have libertie in open Court to advise with any man they thine fitte to resolve or direct them, before they give in their verdict.

77. In all cases wherein any freeman is to give his vote, be it in point of Election, making constitutions and orders or poassing sentence in any case of Judicature or the like, if he cannot see reason to give it positively one way or an other, he shall have libertie to be silent, and not pressed to a determined vote.

78. The Generall or publique Treasure or any parte thereof shall never be expended but by the appointment of a Generall Court, nor any Shire Treasure, but by the appointment of the freemen thereof, nor any Towne Treasurie but by the freemen of that Township.

Liberties of Women

79. If any man at his death shall not leave his wife a competent portion of his estaite, upon just complaint made to the Generall Court she shall be relieved.

80. Everie marryed woeman shall be free from bodilie correction or stripes by her husband, unless it be in his own defense upon her assault. If there be any just cause of correction complaint shall be made to the Authoritie assembled in some Court, from which onely she shall receive it.

Liberties of Children

81. When parents dye intestate, the Elder sonne shall have a doble portion of his whole estate reall and personall, unlesse the Generall Court upon just cause alleadged shall judge otherwise.

82. When parents dye intestate having noe heires males of their bodies their Daughters shall inherit as Copartners, unlesse the Generall Court upon just reason shall judge otherwise.

83. If any parents shall wilfullie and unreasonably deny any childe timely or convenient marriage, or shall exercise any unnaturall severitie towards them, such children shall have free libertie to complaine to Authoritie for redresse.

84. No orphan during their minoritie which was not committed to tuition or service by the parents in their life time, shall afterwards be absolutely disposed of by any kindred, friend, Excecutor, Towneship or Church, nor by themselves without the consent of some Court, wherein two Assistants at least shall be present.

Liberties of Servants

85. If any servants shall flee from the Tiranny and crueltie of their masters to the howse of any freeman of the same Towne, they shall be there protected and susteyned till due order be taken for their relief. Provided due notice thereof be speedily given to their maisters from whom they fled. And the next Assistant or Constable whre the partie flying is harboured.

86. No servant shall be put of for above a yeare to any other neither in the life time of their maiser nor after their

death by their Executors or Adminstrators unlesse it be by consent of Authoritie assembled in some Court or two Assistants.

87. If any man smite out the eye or tooth of his man-servant, or maid servant, or otherwise mayme or much disfigure him, unlesse it be by mere casualtie, he shall let them goe free from his service. And shall have such further recompense as the Court shall allow him.

88. Servants that have served deligentlie and faithfully to the benefit of their maiseters seaven yeares, shall not be sent away emptie. And if any have bene unfaithfull, negligent or unprofitable in their service, notwithstanding the good usage of their maisters, they shall not be dismissed till they have made satisfaction according to the Judgement of Authoritie.

Liberties of Forreiners and Strangers

89. If any people of other Nations professing the true Christian Religion shall flee to us from the Tiranny or oppression of their persecutors, or from famine, warres, or the like necessary and compularie cause, They shall be entertained and succoured amongst us, according to that power and prudence, god shall give us.

90. If any ships or other vessels, be it friend or enemy, shall suffer shipwrack upon our Coast, there shall be no violence or wrong offered to their persons or goods. But their persons shall be harboured, and relieved, and their goods preserved in safety till Authoritie may be certified thereof, and shall take further order therein.

91. There shall never be any bond slaverie, vilinage or Captivitie amongst us unless it be lawfull Captives taken

in just warres, and such strangers as willingly selle
themselves or are sold to us. And these shall have all the
liberties and Christian usages which the law of god
established in Israell concerning such persons doeth
morally require. This exempts none from servitude who
shall be Judged thereto by Authoritie.

Off the Bruite Creature

92. No man shall exercise any Tirrany or Crueltie towards
any bruite Creature which are usuallie kept for man's
use.

93. If any man shall have occasion to leade or drive Cattle
from place to place that is far of, so that they be weary,
or hungrey, or fall sick, or lambe, It shall be lawful to
rest or refresh them, for competent time, in any open
place that is not Corne, meadow, or inclosed for some
peculair use.

94. *Capitall Laws*

1. Deut. 13.6, 19.0. Deut. 17.2,6. Ex. 22.20

If any man after legall conviction shall have or worship
any other god, but the lord god, he shall be put to death.

2. Ex. 22.18. Lev. 20.27. Dut. 18.10

If any man or woeman be a witch, (that is hath or
consulteth with a familiar spirit,) They shall be put to
death.

3. Lev.24.15,16

If any person shall Blaspheme the name of god, the father, Sonne or Holie Ghost, with direct, expresse, presumptuous or high handed blasphemie, or shall curse god in the like manner, he shall be put to death.

4. Ex. 21.12. Numb. 35.13, 14, 20, 31.

If any person commit any wilfull murther, which is manslaughter, committed upon premeditated malice, hatred, or Crueltie, not in a mans necwsaire and just defence, nor by mere casualtie against his will, he shall be put to death.

5. Numb. 25, 20, 21. Lev. 24.17

If any person slayeth an other suddainely in his anger or Crueltie of passion, he shall be put to death.

6. Ex. 21.14

If any person shall slay an other through guile, either by poisoning or other such divelish practice, he shall be put to death.

7. Lev. 20.15, 16.

If any man or woeman shall lye with any beaste or bruite creature by Carnall Copulation, They shall surely be put to death. And the beast shall be slaine, and buried and not eaten.

8. Lev. 20.13.

If any man lyeth with mankinde as he lyeth with a woeman, both of them have committed abhomination, they both shall surely be put to death.

9. Lev. 20.19 and 18, 20. Dut. 22. 23, 24.

If any person committeth Adultery with a married or espoused wife, the Adulterer and Adulteresse shall surely be put to death.

10. Ex. 21.16

If any man stealeth a man or mankinde, he shall surely be put to death.

11. Deut. 19.16, 18, 19.

If any man rise up by false witness, wittingly and of purpose to take away any mans life, he shall be put to death

12. [no Biblical citation listed]

If any man shall conspire and attempt any invasion, insurrection, or publique rebellion against our commonwealth, or shall indeavour to surpirze any Towne or Townes, fort or forts therein, or shall treacherously and perfediouslie attempt the alteration and subversion of our frame of politie or Government fundamentalie, she shall be put to death.

94. *A Declaration of the Liberties the Lord Jesus hath given to the Churches*

1. All the people of god within this Jurisdiction who are not in a church way, and be orthodox in Judgement, and not scandalous in life, shall have full libertie to gather themselves into a Church Estaite. Provided they doe it in a Christian way, with due observation of the rules of Christ revealed in his word.

2. Every Church hath full libertie to exercise all the ordinances of god, according to the rules of scripture.

3. Every Church hath free libertie of Election and ordination of all their officers from time to time, provided they be able, pious and orthodox.

4. Every Church hath free libertie of Admission, Recommendation, Dismisson, and Expulsion, or deposal of their officers, and members, upon due cause, with free exercise of the Discipline and Cenures of Christ according to the rules of his word.

5. No injunctions are to be put upon any Church, Church officers or member in point of Doctrine, worship or Discipline, whether for substance or cercumstance besides the Institutions of the Lord.

6. Every Church of Christ hath freedome to celebrate dayes of fasting and prayer, and of thanksgiveing according to the word of god.

7. The Elders of Churches have free libertie to meete monthly, Quarterly, or otherwise, in convenient numbers and places, for conferences, and consultations about Christian and Church questions and occasions.

8. All Churches have libertie to deale with any of their members in s church way that are in the hand of Justice. So it be not to retard or hinder the course thereof.

9. Every Church hath libertie to deale with any magestrate, Deputie of Court or other officer what soe ever that is a member in a church way in case of

apparent and just offence given in their places, so it be done with due observance and respect.

10. Wee allowe private meetings for edification in religion amongst Christians of all sortes of people. So it be without just offence for number, time, place, and other cercumstance.

11. For the preventing and removeing of errour and offence that may grow and spread in any of the Churches in the Juridiction, And for the preserveing of trueith and peace in the severall churches within themselves, and for the maintenance and exercise of brotherly communion, amongst all the churches in the Countrie, It is allowed and ratifed, by the Authoritie of this Generall Court as a lawfull libertie of the Churches of Christ. They once in every month of the yeare (when the season will beare it) It shall be lawfull for the ministers and Elders, of the Churches neere adjoyneing together, with any other of the breetheren with the consent of the churches to assemble by course in each severall Church one after an other. To the intent after the preching of the word by such a minister as shall be requested thereto by the Elders of the church where the Asembly is held, The rest of the day may be spent in publique Christian Conference about the discussing and resolveing of any such doubts and case of conscience concerning matter of doctrine or worship or government of the church as shall be propounded by any of the Bretheren of that church, will leave also to any other Brother to propound his objections or answeres for further satisfaction according to the word of god. Provided that the whole action be guided and moderated by the Elders of the Church were the

Assemblie is helde, or by such others as they shall appoint. And that no thing be concluded and imposed by way of Authoritie from one or more churches upon an other, but onely by way of Brotherly conference and consultations. That the trueth may be searched out to the satisfying of every mans conscience in the sight of god according his worde. And because such an Assembly and the worke thereof can not be duely attended to if other lectures be held in the same weeke, t is therefore agreed with the consent of the Churches. That in that weeke when such an Assembly is held, All the lectures in all the neighbouring Churches forthat weeke shall be forborne. That so the publique service of Christ in this more solemne Assembly may be transacted with greater deligence and attention.

96. Howsoever these above specified rites, freedoms Immunities, Authorities and priveledges, both Civill and Ecclesiastical are expressed onely under the name and title of Liberties, and not in the exact forme of of Laws or Statutes, yet we do with one consent fullie Authorise, and earnestly intreate all that are and shall be in Authoritie to consider them as laws, and not to faile to inflect condigne and proportionable punishments upon evry man impartiallie, that shall infringe or violate any of them.

97. We likewise give full power and libertie to any person that shall at any time be denyed or deprived of any of them, to commence and prosecute their suite, Complaint or action against any man that shall doe in any Court that hath proper Cognizance or judicature thereof.

98. Lastly because our dutie and desire is to do nothing suddainlie which fundamentally concerne us, we decree

that these rites and liberties, shall be Audably read and deliberately weighed at every Generall Court that shall be held, within three yeares next insueing, And such of them as shall not be alter or repealed they shall stand so ratified, That no man shall infringe them without due punishment.

And if any General Court within these next thre yeares shall faile or forget to reade and consider them as abovesaid, The Governor and Deputy Governor for the time being, and every Assistant present at such Courts, shall forfeite 20sh. A man, and everie Deputie 10sh a man for each neglect, which shall be paid out of their proper estate, and not by the Countrie or the Townes which choose them, and whensoever there shall arise any question in any Court amonge the Assistants and Associates thereof about the explanation of the Rites and liberties, The Generall Court onely shall have the power to interpret them.

[Note: Ward, Nathaniel, Compiler. "Body of Liberties" Collections of the Massachusetts Historical Society, Third Series, Vol. VIII (Boston: MHS, 1843)

The Body of Liberties were written and compiled by Reverend Nathaniel Ward. Ward came to New England in 1634. He was an assistant pastor at Ipswich, Massachusetts. Here he compiled the "Body of Liberties" which were adopted by the General Court of Massachusetts in December, 1641. There is some suspicion that Reverend John Cotton attempted to submit his ideas and changes prior to adoption by the General Court. Apparently, these were rejected.]

The cursed opinions of Anne Hutchinson
From: Thomas Weld's *The Heresies of Anne Hutchinson and Her Followers*
(1644)
(public domain material)

The opinions (some of them) were such as these; I say, some of them, to give but a taste, for afterwards you shall see a litter of fourscore and eleven of their brats hung up against the sun, besides many new ones of Mistress Hutchinson's; all which they hatched and dandled, as:

1. That the Law and the preaching of it, is of no use at all to drive a man to Christ.

2. That a man is united to Christ and justified, without faith; yea, from eternity.

3. That faith is not a receiving of Christ, but a man's discerning that he hath received him already.

4. That a man is united to Christ only by the work of the Spirit upon him, without any act of his.

5. That a man is never effectually Christ's, till he hath assurance.

6. This assurance is only from the witness of the Spirit.

7. This witness of the Spirit is merely immediate, without any respect to the word, or any concurrence with it.

8. When a man hath once this witness he never doubts more.

9. To question my assurance, though I fall into murder or adultery, proves that I never had true assurance.

10. Sanctification can be no evidence of a man's good estate.

11. No comfort can be had from any conditional promise.

12. Poverty in spirit (to which Christ pronounced blessedness, Matt. V.3) is only this, to see I have no grace at all.

13. To see I have no grace in me, will give me comfort; but to take comfort from sight of grace, is legal.

14. An hypocrite may have Adam's graces that he had in innocency.

15. The graces of Saints and hypocrites differ not.

16. All graces are in Christ, as in the subject, and none in us, that Christ believes, Christ loves, etc.

17. Christ is the new Creature.

18. God loves a man never the better for any holiness in him, and never the less, be he never so unholy.

19. Sin in a child of God must never trouble him.

20. Trouble in conscience for sins of Commission, or for neglect of duties, shows a man to be under a covenant of works.

21. All covenants to God expressed in works are legal works.

22. A Christian is not bound to the Law as a rule of his conversation.

23. A Christian is not bound to pray except the Spirit moves him.

24. A minister that hath not this (new) light is not able to edify others; that have it.

25. The whole letter of the Scriptures is a covenant of works.

26. No Christian must be pressed to duties of holiness.

27. No Christian must be exhorted to faith, love, and prayer, etc. except we know he hath the Spirit.

28. A man may have all graces, and yet want Christ.

29. All a believer's activity is only to act sin.

BIBLIOGRAPHY

In addition to the texts and materials used as primary sources and quoted there from, the following is a listing of secondary texts and articles:

General:

Akagi, Roy H. *The Town Proprietors of the New England Colonies.* (Gloucester: Peter Smith), 1924.

Aurand, A. Monroe, Jr. *Bundling in The New World.* (Harrisburg: Aurand P), 1938.

Bercovitch, Sacvan. *The Puritan Origins of the American Self.* (New Haven: Yale UP), 1975.

_____ *The American Jeremiad.* (Madison: University of Wisconsin Press), 1978.

Breen, T. H. *The Character of the Good Ruler.* (New Haven: Yale UP), 1970.

Bremer, Francis J. *Congregational Communion.* (Boston: Northeastern UP), 1994.

Brown, Richard B. *Massachusetts, A History.* (NY: W.W. Norton), 1972.

Fischer, David H. *Albion's Seed.* (NY: Oxford UP), 1989.

Hall, Michael Garibaldi. *Edward Randolph and the American Colonies, 1776-1703*. (Chapel Hill: University of North Carolina P) 1960.

Hart, Albert, Ed., *The Commonwealth History of Massachusetts, 5 Vols.* (NY: States History Co.), 1927-1930.

Hayek, F.A. *The Constitution of Liberty*. (Chicago: University of Chicago P), 1960.

Ingebretsen, Ed. *Maps of Heaven, maps of hell*. (Armonk: M.E. Sharpe), 1996.

Kaufmann, Michael W. *Institutional Individualism*. (Hanover: UP of New England), 1998.

Lovejoy, David S. "Between Hell and Plum Island: Samuel Sewall and the Legacy of the Witches, 1692-97." *New England Quarterly* 70.3 (Sep 1997): 355-68.

Marin, John F. *Profits in the Wilderness*. (Chapel Hill: UNCP), 1991.

Matthews, William. *American Diaries in Manuscript*. (Athens: University of Georgia P) 1974.

Morgan, Edmund S. *Puritan Political Ideas*. (Indianapolis: Bobbs-Merrill), 1965.

Oberholzer, Emil. *Delinquent Saints*. (NY: Columbia UP), 1956.

Powell, Sumner C. *Puritan Village: The Formation of a New England Town*. (NY: Doubleday), 1966.

Schneider, Herbert W. *The Puritan Mind.* (U of Michigan P), 1958.

Schweninger, Lee. *John Winthrop.* (Boston: Twayne), 1990.

Shahar, Shulamith.   *The Fourth Estate.*   (London: Routledge), 1991.

Weeden, William B. *Economic and Social History of New England, 1620-1789, Vols. I & II.* (NY: Hillary House), 1890.

Native People and the Colonial Period:

Allen, David G. *In English Ways.* (Chapel Hill: University of North Carolina press), 1981.

Cronon, William. *Changes in the Land: Indians, Colonists, and the Ecology of New England.* (New York: Oxford UP), 1983.

Morison, Samuel E. *Builders of the Bay Colony.* (Boston: Houghton Mifflin), 1958.

Death and Burial:

Alexis, Gerhard T. "Wiggleworth's 'Easiest Room,'" *New England Quarterly,* 42 (Dec, 1969)

Henson, Robert. "Form and Content of the Puritan Funeral Elegy." *American Literature,* 32.1 (1960).

Moran, Gerald and Maris Vinovskis. "Angels' Heads and Weeping Willows: Death in Early America." *Religion, Family, and the Life Course.* (Ann Arbor: University of Michigan P), 1992.

Cultural and Social:

Adams, William. *The Diary of William Adams.* (Boston: Massachusetts Historical Society, Collections, *IV,* I).

Bosco, Ronald A. *The Poems of Michael Wigglesworth.* (Landham: University Press of America), 1989.

Bradstreet, Simon. *The Diary of Simon Bradstreet.* (Boston: New England Historic Genealogical Register), October, 1854.

Clap, Roger. *Memoirs of Captain Roger Clap.* (Boston: n.p.), 1731. (reprinted by R. &. S. Draper), 1766.

Cunningham, Hugh. *Children and Childhood in Western Society since 1500.* (London: Longman), 1995.

Danforth, Samuel, Rev. *The Diary of Samuel Danforth.* (Boston: New England Historic Genealogical Register), Jan., Apr., July, and Oct., 1880.

Danforth, Samuel (son of above). *The Diary of Samuel Danforth, Jr.* (Boston: New England Historic Genealogical Register), July, 1853.

Eliot, John. *The Diary of Reverend John Eliot.* (Boston: New England Historic Genealogical Register), 1879.

Green, Joseph. *The Commonplace Book of Joseph Green (1675-1715).* (NY: AMS Press), 1943.

Hambrick-Stowe, Charles E. (Ed.) *Early New England Meditative Poetry: Anne Bradstreet and Edward Taylor.* (NY: Paulist Press), 1988.

Hawes, Joseph M. and N. Ray Hiner, Editors. *American Childhood.* (Westport: Greenwood Press), 1985.

Jones, Serene. *Calvin and the Rhetoric of Piety* (Louisville: Westminster John Know P), 1995.

Lechford, Thomas. *Plain Dealing: or News from New England.* (New York: Johnson Reprint Corp), 1969.

Macfarlane, Alan, ed. *The Diary of Ralph Josselin, 1616-1683.* (NY: Oxford UP), 1976.

Newberry, Benjamin. *The Diary of Benjamin Newberry.* (Boston: Magazine of New England History, Vol. III).

Piercy, Josephine K. *Anne Bradstreet.* (New York: Twayne P), 1965.

Scheick, William J. *The Will and the Word: The Poetry of Edward Taylor.* (Athens: U of Georgia P) 1974.

Smith, John E, Harry S. Stout, and Kenneth P. Minkema, editors. *A Jonathan Edwards Reader.* (New Haven: Yale UP), 1995.

Smith, Josiah. *Doctrine and Glory of the Saints' Resurrection.* (Boston: S. Kneeland and T. Green), 1742.

Spalding, Ruth, ed. *The Diary of Bulstrode Whitelocke.* (NY: Oxford UP), 1990.

Stavely, Keith W.F. *Puritan Legacies: Paradise Lost and the New England Tradition, 1630-1890.* (Ithaca: Cornell UP), 1987.

Thompson, Roger. *Sex in Middlesex.* (Amherst: University of Massachusetts Press), 1986.

Wish, Harvey. *The Diary of Samuel Sewell.* (NY: G.P. Putnam's Sons), 1967.

Puritan Beliefs and Practices:

Caldwell, Patricia. *The Puritan Conversion Narrative.* (Cambridge: Cambridge UP), 1983.

Cable, Mary. *The Little Darlings: A History of Child Rearing in America.* (NY: Scribner), 1975.

Greven, Philip J. Jr., *Child-rearing Concepts, 1628-1861.* (Itasca: F.E. Peacock), 1973.

Mather, Cotton. *Baptismal Piety.* (Boston: n.p.), 1727.

McGrath, Alister E. *The Intellectual Origins of the Reformation.* (London: Oxford UP), 1987.

Religion:

Baxter, Richard. *Plain Scripture Proof of Infants Church-Membership and Baptism.* (London: Printed for Robert White), 1651.

Cotton, John. *The New Covenant, or, A Treatise, unfolding the order and manner of the giving and receiving of the Covenant of Grace to the Elect.* (London: Printed by M.S. for Francis Eglesfield and John Allen), 1654.

_____, *Showing the Difference Between the Legallist and the True Christian.* (London: Printed by M.S.), 1654.

Danforth, Samuel. *The Duties of Believers.* (Boston, n.p.), 1708.

Dillenberger, John, (ed.) *John Calvin: Selections from His Writings.* (Missoula: Scholars Press for the American Academy of Religion), 1975.

Eliot, John. *A Brief Answer.* (Boston: n.p.), 1679.

_____, *Propriety of Attending Public Worship.* (Boston: John Russell), 1800.

Hall, David D., ed. *The Antinomian Controversy, 1636-1638.* 2nd ed. (Durham: Duke University Press), 1990.

_____*The Faithful Shepherd: A History of the New England Ministry in the Seventeenth Century.* (Chapel Hill: U of North Carolina P), 1972.

Hooker, Thomas. *"No Man Can Will Christ and Grace."* Redemption: Three Sermons. Ed. Everett H. Emerson. (NY: Scholars' Facsimiles and Reprints), 1977.

Kibbey, Anne. *The Interpretation of Material Shapes in Puritanism: A Study of Rhetoric, Prejudice, and Violence.* (Cambridge: Cambridge UP), 1986.

Mather, Cotton. *Ornaments for the Daughters of Zion.* (Boston, n.p.), 1741.

Packer, J. I. *A Quest for Godliness: The Puritan Vision of the Christian.* (Wheaton: Crossway Books), 1990.

Palmer, Edwin H. *The Five Points of Calvinism.* (Grand Rapids: Baker Book House), 1972.

Perkins, William. *The Order of the Causes of Salvation and Damnation.* (London, n.p.) 1608.

Pettit, Norman. *The Heart Prepared: Grace and Conversion in Puritan Spiritual Life.* (Middletown: Wesleyan UP), 1978.

Pope John Paul II. *Immaculate Conception Defined by Pius IX.* http://www.goarch.org/access/html

Shepard, Thomas. *The Sincere Convert.* (Cambridge, n.p.), 1664.

Taylor, Jeremy. *State of Man in This Life.* (Boston: T. Fleet), 1723.

Underdown, David. *Fire from Heaven.* (New Haven: Yale UP), 1992.

Walter, Nehemiah. *Sorrows and the Desires of the Regenerate.* (Boston: John Draper), 1736.

_____, *Unfruitful Hearers Detected and Warned. (Boston, n.p.) n.d.).*

Weld, Thomas. *The Perfect Pharisee Under Monkish Holiness.* (London: S.B.), 1653.

BIBLIOGRAPHY AND NOTES FOR THE EPILOGUE BY DR. LITA LINZER SCHWARTZ

Beals, R.W., Jr. (1975) In search of the historical child: miniature adulthood and youth in colonial New England. American Quarterly, 27, 379-398.

Belleck, P. (2001, July 27) Many states ceding regulations to church groups. The New York Times, pp. A1, A14.

Borick, B. (2001) Wide as the Waters. New York: Simon & Schuster.

Breen, T. H., &Foster, S. (1973). The Puritan's greatest achievement: A study of social cohesion in 17th century Massachusetts. Journal of American History, 60 (1) 5-22.

Cable, M. (1975). The Little Darlings: A history of children rearing in America. New York: Scribner.

Colarusso, C.A., & Nemiroff, R.A. (1981) Adult development: A new dimension in psychodynamic theory and practice. New York: Plenum.

Cook, L.J. (1998). Katherine Nanny, alias Naylor: A life in Puritan Boston, Historical Archaeology, 32 (1) 15-19.

Courtwright, D.T. (1985). New England families in historical perspective. Dublin Seminar for New England Folklife Annual Proceedings. 10, pp. 11-23.

Demos, John. (2000). A Little Commonwealth. New York: Oxford University Press.

Erikson, E. H. (1963). Childhood and society, 2nd ed. New York: W.W. Norton.

Harevan, T. K. (1991). The history of the family and the complexity of social change. The American Historical Review, 96 (1), 95-124.

Harper, G.W. (1994). New England dynasty: The lives and legacies of the Mathers, America's most influential Puritan family. Christian History, 13, 20-22.

Kaestle, C.F. & Vinovskis, M.A. (1978). From apron strings to ABCs: Parents, children, and schooling in Nineteenth-century Massachusetts. American Journal of Sociology, 84 (Supplement), S39-S80.

Kephart, W.M. & Zellner, W.W. (1991). Extraordinary groups: An examination of unconventional life-styles, 4th ed. New York: St. Martin's Press.

Kett, J.F. (1978) Curing the disease of precocity. American Journal of Sociology, 84 (Supplement), S183-S211.

Langone, M. D., & Eisenberg, G. (1993). Church and cults. In M.D. Langone (Ed.) Recovery from cults: Help for victims of psychological and spiritual abuse (pp. 327-342). New York: W.W. Norton.

Leverenz, D. (1980) The Language of Puritan Feeling. New Brunswick, NJ: Rutgers University Press.

Lewin, K. (1954). Behavior and development as a function of the total situation. In L. Carmichael, (Ed.), Manual of Child Psychology, 2nd ed. (pp.918-970). New York: John Wiley.

Marrow, A.J. (1977). The Practical Theorist: The life and work of Kurt Lewin. New York: Teachers College Press.

Saveth, E.N. (1969), "The Problem of American Family History." American Quarterly, 21 (Issue 2, Part 2) Supplement), 311-329.

Schwartz, L.L. (1969). American Education: A problem-centered approach. Boston: Holbrook Press.

Schwartz, L.L. & Kaslow, F.W. (1982). The cult phenomenon: Historical, sociological, and familial factors contributing to the development and appeal. In F. Kaslow & M.B. Sussman, Eds., Cults and the Family, pp. 3-30. New York: Haworth Press.

Slater, P.G. (1997). Children in the New England Mind in Death and in Life. Hamden, CN" Archon Books.

Somerville, C. J. (1992) The Discovery of Childhood in Puritan England. Athens, GA: University of Georgia Press.

Street, W.R. (1994). <u>A Chronology of Noteworthy Events in American Psychology.</u> Washington, D.C. American Psychological Association.

Swinford, S.P., DeMaris, A., Cernkovich, S.A., & Giordano, P.C. (2000). Harsh physical discipline in childhood and violence in later romantic involvements: The mediating role of problem behaviors. <u>Journal of Marriage & the Family, 62,</u> 508-519.

Ulrich, L.T. <u>Good Wives</u>. (1991) New York: Vintage Books.

[Note: Profound thanks to my good friend and colleague, Natalie Isser, Ph.D., Professor Emerita of History, Pennsylvania State University, who shared her knowledge of historical events and sources with me.]

NOTES

[1] Moran, Gerald F. and Vinovski, Maris A. "The Puritan Family and Religion" William and Mary Quarterly. 39: 29-63 (1982)

[2] Foster, Stephen, *Their Solitary Way* (New Haven: Yale UP, 1971), 1.

[3] Foster, 1.

[4] Packer, J. I. *A Quest for Godliness: The Puritan Vision of the Christian* (Wheaton: Crossway Books, 1990) 284.

[5] Ellerbe, Helen, *The Dark Side of Christian History* (FL: Morningstar and Lark, 1995), 98.

[6] Pagels, Elaine, *Adam, Eve, and the Serpent* (NY: Random House, 1958), 131-4.

[7] Armstrong, Karen, *A History of God* (NY: Ballantine Books, 1993), 123-4.

[8] Spong, John, *Why Christianity Must Change or Die* (SF: HarperCollins, 1999), 86-7.

[9] www.religiontolerance.org/virgin-b.htm

[10] religiontolerance, 19.

[11] Seeburg, Augustine R., *History of Doctrine, Vol. I* (Grand Rapids: Baker Book House, 1954), 343.

[12] Harnack, Adolf, *History of Dogma, Vol. V* (NY: Russell & Russell, 1958), 227.

[13] Seeburg, I, 344.

[14] Seeburg, Vol. II, 399.

[15] Strong, A.H., *Systematic Theology* (Old Tappan: Fleming H. Revell, 1969), 625.

[16] Webster, Samuel, *A Winter Evening's Conversation Upon the Doctrine of Original Sin* (Boston, 1757), 6,28.

[17] Wish, Harvey, *The Diary of Samuel Sewell* (NY: G.P. Putnam's Sons, 1967), 85.

[18] Smith, John E, Harry S. Stout, and Kenneth P. Minkema, editors, *A Jonathan Edwards Reader* (New Haven: Yale UP, 1995) 95.

[19] Smith, et al, vii.

[20] A Report of the Records Commissioners, 2nd Edition, (Boston: Rockwell and Churchill, Printers, 1884), 145-146.

[21] Edwards, Jonathan, "The Justice of God in the Damnation of Sinner," from *The Works of Jonathan Edwards, A.M.* (London: Henry G. Bohn, 1845) 673.

[22] Delbanco, Andrew, *The Puritan Ordeal* (Cambridge: Harvard UP, 1989), 46.

[23] Downame, John, *The Christian Warfare Against the Devil, World, and Flesh* (London, np, 1633), 16.

[24] Downame, 45.

[25] Perkins, William, *The Order of the Causes of Salvation and Damnation* (London, np, 1608) 31.

[26] Bremer, Francis J., *The Puritan Experiment* (Hanover: UP New England, 1995), 18.

[27] Walter, Nehemiah, *Sorrows and the Desires of the Regenerate* (Boston, John Draper, 1736) 4.

[28] Walter, 13.

[29] Eliot, John, *New England's First Fruits with Divers Other Special Matters Concerning That Country* (London: R.O. and G.D., 1643), 6,7, 16.

[30] Walter, 19.

[31] Walter, 24.

[32] Watson, Thomas, *The Mischief of Sin* (London, Thomas Parhurst, 1671), 1.2.

[33] Watson, 33.

[34] Watson, 92-100.

[35] Watson, 4-9.

[36] Pierson, Paul, *Historical Development of the Christian Movement.* Audio Tape 12.0.

[37] Delbanco, 55.

[38] Fleming, 79.

[39] Sibbes, Richard, *A Description of Christ* (London: 1620), 10.

[40] Mather, Cotton, *A Family Well-Ordered* (Boston: B. Green and J. Allen, 1699), 28-9.

[41] Daniels, Bruce C., *Puritans at Play* (NY: St. Martin's Griffin, 1995), 166.

[42] Ulrich, Laurel Thatcher, *Good Wives* (New York: Vintage Books, 1991), 156.

[43] www.Christianitytoday.com/holidays/thanksgiving/features/41h041htm

[44] Thompson, Roger, *Sex in Middlesex* (Amherst: University of Massachusetts Press, 1986) 103.

[45] Thompson, 103.

[46] Middlekauff, Robert, *The Mathers* (London: Oxford University Press,1971), 126.

[47] Mather, Cotton, *The Duties of Parents to their Children.* (Boston, np, n.d.), 2.

[48] Mather, 4.

[49] Mather, 8.

[50] Mather, 10.

[51] Mather, 15.

[52] Rowlandson, Joseph, *A Manifesto or Declaration Set Forth by the Undertakers of the New Church* (Boston, np, 1699), 9.

[53] Miller, Perry, *The New England Mind: From Colony to Province* (Cambridge: Harvard UP, 1953), 254.

[54] Miller, 255.

[55] Morgan, Edmund S., *Visible Saints* (NY: NYUP, 1963), 124-5.

[56] Morgan, 132.

[57] Shepard, Thomas, *The Church Membership of Children and Their Right to Baptisme* (Cambridge, np, 1663), 13-4.

[58] Morgan, 137.

[59] Ellis, George E., *The Puritan Commonwealth: Its Basis, Organization and Administration* (Boston: James Osgood, 1880), I, 166.

[60] Calvin, John, *Institutes of the Christian Religion (1559), I: IV:* Ford Lewis Battles, translator. (PA: Westminister Press, 1960), II: 1022-23.

[61] Walker, Williston, Ed., "*Results of the Synod of 1662, The Creeds and Platforms of Congregationalism* (NY: United Church Press, [1893] reprinted, 1960), 328.

[62] Bradshaw, William, *A Preparation to the Receiving of Christ's Body and Blood: Directing the weake Christians How They May Worthily Receive the Same* (Boston, n.p, 1630), 94.

[63] Bradshaw, 105.

[64] Bradshaw, 5.

[65] Delbanco, 224.

[66] Morgan, Edmund S., *Visible Saints* (NY: NYYP, 1963), 133.

[67] Mather, Increase, *The First Principles of New England* (Cambridge: Samuel Green, 1675), 10-11.

[68] Delbanco, 230.

[69] Pope, Robert G., *The Half-Way Covenant* (Princeton: PUP, 1969), 210-211.

[70] Pope, 279.

[71] Miller, 490.

[72] Washburn, Emory, *Sketches of Judicial History of Massachusetts* (Boston: Little and Brtown, 1840), 31.

[73] Washburn, 35.

[74] Washburn, 40.

[75] Hilkey, Charles J., *Legal Development in Colonial Massachusetts.* (NY: Longemans, Green, 1910), 60.

[76] Johnson, Gerald G., *The Biography and Genealogy of Captain John Johnson from Roxbury, Massachusetts* (Bowie: Heritage Books, 2000), 170-171.

[77] Erikson, Kai, *Wayward Puritans* (NY: John Wiley and Sons, 1966), 12.

[78] Boston Sermons, January 14, 1671-2.

[79] Winthrop, John, *The Winthrop Journal* (Boston: Massachusetts Historical Society, 1956), 378.

[80] Dow, George F., *Everyday Life in the Massachusetts Bay Colony* (Boston: Society for the Preservation of New England Antiquities, 1935), 225-6.

[81] Walker, 423-31.

[82] Walker, 430.

[83] Sewell, Samuel, *The Diary of Samuel Sewell, edited by M. Halsey Thomas* (NY: Farrar, Straus, and Giroux, 1973), I, 141.

[84] Sewell, 310.

[85] Sewell, 282.

[86] *Roxbury Land and Church Records, A report of the Record Commissioners of Boston* (Boston: Rockwell and Churchill, City Printers, 1884) 98.

[87] Sewell, 70.

[88] Sewell, 69.

[89] Publications of the Colonial Society of Massachusetts, Volume XXIX, Collections (Boston: Published by the Society, 1933) 265.

[90] Ibid., 409.

[91] Ibid., 113.

[92] Ibid., 1163.

[93] Sewell, 23.

[94] Hambleton, Else L., *"Sex and Sexuality in Early America"* Turning Points: Essays on the Family (Chicago: UCP, 1978), 98.

[95] Aurand, A. Monroe, *Bundling in the New World* (Harrisburg: Aurand Press, 1938) 12.

[96] Ulrich, 103.

[97] Winslow,

[98] Ford, Paul L., *The New England Primer* (NY: Dodd, Mead, 1899), 19.

[99] Ford, 24.

[100] Cotton, John, *"A Catechism" from A Survey of the Sum of Church Discipline, 1646. Public Domain.*

[101] Cotton, John, *Spiritual Milk for Babes Drawn Out of the Breasts of both Testaments for Their Souls Nourishment. (1645)* (Public Domain)

[102] Diary of Samuel Sewall, Vol. V, Proceedings of the Massachusetts Historical Society, 2nd Series (1884-5) (Boston), 469.

[103] Stannard, David E., *The Puritan Way of Death* (NY: Oxford UP, 1977), 45.

[104] Weber, Max, translated by Talcott Parsons. *The Protestant Ethic and Spirit of Capitalism* (NY: Scribner, 1958), 104.

[105] Stannard, 47.

[106] Stannard, 205.

[107] Slater, Peter G., *Children in the New England Mind* (Hamden: Archon Book, 1977), 117.

[108] Stannard, 171.

[109] Mather, Increase, *Pray for the Rising Generation* (Boston, n.p., 1678), 62-3.

[110] Ford, 34.

[111] Norton, John, *A Discussion of that Great Point in Divinity, the Suffering of Christ* (London, n.p., 1653), 2,7.

[112] Shea, William R., *"Galileo and the Church"*, in Lindberg and Numbers, editors. *God and Nature,* 125.

[113] Mather, I., 22.

[114] Fleming, Sanford, *Children and Puritism* (New Haven: YUP, 1933), 103.

[115] Fleming, 133.

[116] Shepard, 43.

[117] Wigglesworth, Michael, *The Day of Doom* (Public Domain), 23.

[118] Wigglesworth, 43.

[119] Wigglesworth, 35.

[120] Wigglesworth, 45.

[121] Wigglesworth, 52.

[122] Mather, C., 76.

[123] Fleming, 68.

[124] Stannard, 109.

[125] Stannard, 115.

[126] Geddes, Gordon E., *Welcome Joy* (Ann Arbor: UMI Research Press, 1976), 118.

[127] Mather, Cotton, *Magnalia Christi Americana I,* 578 (Public Domain).

[128] A Report of the Record Commissioners containing the Roxbury Land and Church Records (2nd Edition; (Boston: Rockwell and Churchill, City Printers, 1884), 75.

[129] Stannard, 117.

[130] Oliver, Peter, *The Puritan Commonwealth* (Boston: Little, Brown, 1856), 193

[131] www.ecu.edu/polsci/hough/2Puritan.htm

[132] Gaustad, Edwin C., *Liberty of Conscience* (Grand Rapids: William B. Eerdmans, 1991), 219.

[133] Middlekauff, Robert, *The Mathers* (London: Oxford UP, 1971), 213.

[134] Holliday, Carl, *Woman's Life in Colonial Days* (Boston: Cornhill, 1992), 40.

[135] Baltzell, E. Digby, *Puritan Boston and Quaker Philadelphia* (NY: The Free Press, 1979), 136.

[136] Weld, Thomas, *The Heresies of Anne Hutchinson and Her Followers.* (Public Domain)

[137] Weld, Thomas, *Twenty-nine Cursed Opinions* (London, np, 1644).

[138] Miller, Perry, *The New England Mind: From Colony to Province.* (Cambridge: Harvard UP, 1953), 485.

[139] Rutman, Darrett B., *Winthrop's Boston* (NY: Norton, 1965), 119-120.

[140] North, Gary, *Puritan Economic Experiments* (Fort Worth: Dominion Press, 1988), 52.

[141] North, 58.

[142] Bremer, Francis J., *The Puritan Experiment* (Hanover: UP New England, 1995), 213.

[143] Preston, John, *The Breast Plate of Faith and Love* (London: R.Y. for Nicholas Bourne, 1634), I, 31-32.

[144] Preston, 32.

[145] Ames, William, *The Works of William Ames* (London: printed for John Rothwell, 1643), 208-211.

[146] Ames, 18.

[147] Preston, 189-190.

[148] Alleine, Joseph, *An Alarm to the Unconverted* (Charlestown: Samuel Etheridge, 1807), 140.

[149] Alleine, 143.

[150] Morgan, 91.

[151] Slater, 148.

[152] Toulouse, Teresa, *The Art of Prophesying* (Athens: University of Georgia Press, 1987), 2.

[153] Toulouse, 2.

[154] Whittingham, William, *The Geneva Bible, reprint.* (Madison: UWP, 1969), 24.

[155] Hatch, Nathan O. and Noll, Mark A. *The Bible in America* (NY: Oxford UP, 1982), 25.

[156] Haskins, George L., *Law and Authority in Early Massachusetts, A Study in Tradition and Design* (NY: MacMillan , 1960), 162.

[157] Hatch and Noll, 22.

[158] Hatch and Noll, 22.

[159] Teeple, Howard M., *The Historical Approach to the Bible* (Evanston: Religion and Ethics Institute, 1982), 67.

[160] Teeple, 67.

[161] Johnson, Elliott., *Expository Hemeneutics: An Introduction* (Grand Rapids: Zondervan, 1990), 9.

[162] Toulouse, 189.

[163] Chouinard, Larry, *Christian Standard (10/13/96)., 4.*

[164] Chouinard, 3.

[165] Toulouse, 188.

[166] Toulouse, 188.

[167] Marsden, George A., *Reforming Fundamentalism* (Grand Rapids: W.B. Eerdsmans, 1987) 56.

[168] Willis, Rick, *Prophetic Voice* (Cincinnati: Gospel Truth Ministries, 1999) 2.

[169] Quoted in Kaufmann, Michael W. *Instututional Individualism* (Hanover: Wesleyan University P, 1998) 21.

[170] Kaufmann, 21.

[171] Mather, 23.

[172] Pollock, Linda A., *Forgotten Children* (Cambridge: CUP, 1983), 269.

[173] Fischer, David H., *Albion's Seed* (NY: Oxford UP, 1989), 100.

[174] Slater, 119.

[175] Lockridge, Kenneth A., *A New England Town* (NY: Norton, 1970), 67.

[176] Edwards, Charles E., *"Calvin on Infant Salvation"* Bibliothera Sacra, 88, 1931), 328.

[177] Rutman, 152.

[178] Slater, 103.

[179] Ulrich, 158.

[180] Morgan, Edmund S., *The Puritan Family.* (NY: Harper & Row, 1966), 25.

[181] Morgan, 103.

[182] Schucking, Levin L., *The Puritan Family* (NY: Schocken Books, 1969), 75.

[183] Thornton, John W., *Lives of Isaac Heath and John Bowles and of Rev. John Eliot, Jr.* (Roxbury: Private Distribution, 1850), 49-53.

[184] Thorton, 52.

[185] Thornton, 52.

[186] Schucking, 76.

[187] Daniels, Bruce C., *Puritans at Play* (NY: St. Martin's Griffin, 1995), 14.

[188] Daniels, 14.

[189] Morgan, 78.

[190] http://www.geocities.com/CollegePark/Square/5784/unit 1.htm

[191] Demos, John, American Journal of Sociology, 84: S148.

[192] Fischer, 75.

[193] Brigham, William, *The Compact with the Charter and Laws of the Colony* (Boston: Dutton & Wentworth, 1836), 44.

[194] Slater, 97.

[195] Slater, 16

[196] Slater, 112.

[197] Kaufmann, 109.

[198] Middlekauff, 195.

[199] Powers, Edwin, *Crime and Punishment in Early America: A Documentary History* (Boston: Beacon Press, 1966), 236.

[200] Journal of John Winthrop. Massachusetts Historical Society, 2:83 [1642].

[201] Eldridge, Larry D., *"Crazy-Brained: Mental Illness in Colonial America"* Bulletin of the History of Medicine 70.3, John Hopkins University Press, 1996), 363.

[202] Wish, 32.

[203] Wish, 33.

[204] Suffolk County Records, 1673.

[205] Eldridge, 381.

[206] Eldridge, 384.

[207] *The Diary of Samuel Sewell.*, I. 16.

[208] Sewell, I, 93.

[209] Sewell, I, 321.

[210] Suffolk County Records. Publications, The Colonial Society of Massachusetts (Boston: Published by the Society, 1933) 436.

[211] Cole, Phyllis, *Mary Moody Emerson and the Origins of Transcendentalism.* (NY: Oxford UP, 1998), 22.

[212] Leverenz, David, *The Language of Puritan Feeling* (New Brunswick: Rutgers UP, 1980), 3.

[213] Leverenz, 45.

[214] Cole, 21.

[215] Cole, 21.

[216] Leverenz, 100.
[217] Dod, John and Cleaver, Robert, *A Godlye Form of Household Government*. Quoted in Leverenz, 71.
[218] Cole, 69.
[219] Cole, 69.
[220] Leverenz, 76.
[221] Wish, jacket
[222] Leverenz, 113.
[223] Thompson, 104-5.
[224] www.rickross.com/reference/king/king14.html, 1
[225] www.rickross.com/reference/king/king14.html, 1

INDEX

276

278